ALSO BY PATRICK F. MCMANUS

Kid Camping from Aiii to Zip

A Fine and Pleasant Misery

They Shoot Canoes, Don't They?

Never Sniff a Gift Fish

The Grasshopper Trap

Rubber Legs and White Tail-Hairs

The Night the Bear Ate Goombaw

Whatchagot Stew
(With Patricia "The Troll" McManus Gass)

Real Ponies Don't Go Oink!

The Good Samaritan Strikes Again

How I Got This Way

Never Cry Arp!

Into the Twilight, Endlessly Grousing

The Deer on a Bicycle:
Excursions into the Writing of Humor

The Bear
in the Attic

The Bear in the Attic

PATRICK F. MCMANUS

An Owl Book

Henry Holt and Company   New York

Henry Holt and Company, LLC
Publishers since 1866
115 West 18th Street
New York, New York 10011

Henry Holt® is a registered trademark of
Henry Holt and Company, LLC.

All of the stories in this book previously appeared in slightly
different form in *Outdoor Life* magazine, with the exception of
"The Bear in the Attic" and "Real Work."

Library of Congress Cataloging-in-Publication Data

McManus, Patrick F.
The bear in the attic / Patrick F. McManus.—1st ed.
p. cm.
ISBN 0-8050-7295-0 (pbk.)
1. American wit and humor. I. Title.
PN6165.M39 2002
814'.6—dc21   2002019648

Henry Holt books are available for special
promotions and premiums.
For details contact: Director, Special Markets.

First published in hardcover in 2002 by Henry Holt and Company

First Owl Books Edition 2003

An Owl Book

Designed by Paula Russell Szafranski

Printed in the United States of America

1   3   5   7   9   10   8   6   4   2

Contents

Contents

The Bear
in the Attic

The Bear in the Attic

The little girl rattled on ceaselessly and seamlessly, the lack of even the slightest pause relieving me of any need to respond or, mercifully, to listen. Mostly, she talked to the teddy bear that sat alongside her in the backseat of the car, strapped in with its own seat belt. In a moment of mild insanity, or possibly only laxity of alertness, I had been beguiled into baby-sitting the little girl while her mother and grandmother went shopping. Her name was Devon. She was a nice little girl, very pretty and I think quite bright, perhaps too much so. I felt sorry for her, having a grandmother and mother so irresponsible as to leave her in my care. That's the problem with women these days, no sense of responsibility. Their civility could use a bit of touching up, too, if you ask me. Well, I had predicted this eventual turn of events. Once they get shoes and escape from the kitchen, I said, they'll take over the world and . . .

"Grampa! I'm talking to you!"

"Hunh? Oh, sorry, Devon. I was distracted there for moment. What is it?"

"I said Teddy and I really liked the pool hall. Can we go there again sometime?"

"Perhaps, darlin', perhaps. But we don't call it a pool hall, do we now? What is it we call it?"

"The library!"

"That's right, sweetheart, the library."

"I really liked that big black man who let me sit up on the counter and mixed me Shirley Temples to drink."

"Yes, Ernie's a very nice man. He's the head librarian. Now, why don't you tell your bear a story? I bet he would love to hear you tell him a story. I would, too."

"No! I want you to tell us both a story."

"Oh, I would much prefer that you told the story."

"Pool hall!"

"But if you really want me to, I guess I could. What would you like the story to be about?"

"A bear! Do you know any stories about a bear?"

"A bear. Why, yes, come to think of it, I do. If you would just shut—be really quiet for a few minutes, dear, while Grampa concentrates, I'll even show you where the story took place."

It had been years since I'd driven out to Birchwood, partly because it made me sad to do so. Many of the fine old homes of the early timber barons had now been turned into apartment houses. The occupants of others had adorned the spacious lawns with an assortment of broken automobiles and discarded appliances, a style of landscape design I like to think of as North Idaho Gothic. A few had simply been abandoned to the whims and guiles of the weather. The majestic birches that gave the neighborhood its name were gone, too, cut down because of disease or possibly the need for firewood. Birchwood reminded me of a dog I'd once owned. As a puppy, he was completely white with a brown tip on his tail. When he grew up, the tip vanished, and so we were always explaining to visitors why we had named him Tippy. The present residents of Birchwood no doubt were forever making similar explanations about the name of their neighborhood. Birchwood didn't have a birch in sight.

At last we came to the mansion of my aunt Lucy and uncle Charles Winslow, which wasn't a mansion really but what had seemed like one to me when I was growing up on a tiny stump farm a few miles away. While my family raised essentially the same crop of stumps each year, Uncle Charles and Aunt Lucy wallowed in wealth, "wallow" being my mother's word for describing the affluence of her brother and sister-in-law. If some porcine connotation clings to the word, it was perhaps unintended on Mom's part. Indeed, the Winslows were more than generous with our family, the more so after my father died. Heaping charity upon us at every opportunity, they gave till it hurt, yet another innocent cruelty with which to afflict the poor.

Uncle Charles was an executive, perhaps even the president for all I know, of a timber company, by far the largest establishment in all of Blight County. I'm not sure whether Blight City ever produced a high society as such, but if so, Uncle Charles and Aunt Lucy surely must have enjoyed a lofty perch in it.

"Oh!" exclaimed Devon. "Is that it? Is that the house? It looks terrible! Is it haunted?"

If a ghost still resided in the old Victorian, it would have been the only inhabitant in a long while. Windows were broken out, the front door hung from a single hinge, and a squadron of swallows appeared to be flying sorties from a base in the living room. The attic window remained intact. I glanced at it, then quickly away, not wishing to glimpse anything behind its leaded glass.

"I personally saw only one ghost there," I told Devon. "I doubt it's still around. We could go in and see, if you like."

"No! Just tell the story!"

"Oh, all right. It's kind of scary, though. I don't want your mother and grandmother yelling at me, because you refuse to go to sleep without the light on. Promise not to blab?"

"I promise. Now tell the darn story!"

"The story starts with my cousin Chucky," I began.

"I thought it was about a bear."

"It is about a bear. We get to the bear later. First, I have to tell you about Chucky."

As I explained to Devon, I must confess here that I personally did not witness all the events in this report. I was on hand for many of them, though, and have scrupulously maintained the highest degree of accuracy in reporting whatever I personally witnessed. Over the years I have also accumulated numerous firsthand accounts from various other participants and observers, many of whom had slipped into the grip of compulsive if not pathological reminiscence, usually an unbearable bore but in this instance quite useful. Eventually, all the recollections and bits and chunks of information reached critical mass and melded into the following account, beginning with my cousin Chucky, as I indicated to Devon.

Chucky must have been eight years older than I, because I had just finished doing a stretch in fifth grade when Chucky turned eighteen—draft age! It was 1942 with World War Two still accelerating toward full momentum. I loved that war. Well, I loved it after I became fairly certain we were going to win it. Years later, as I myself approached draft age, I began to see the folly of sending youth such as myself off to foreign lands to risk life and limb. At the time of this memoir, however, I was still enamored of war.

Now here's what I thought was so unfair. I loved the war, Chucky hated it, but he's the one who got to go, scooped up by the draft to be blown off to some great adventure in exotic lands. My cousin was a pale, puffy fellow, with sparse blond hair and fat red lips, the kind of pouty lips a girl might love, if they were attached to her face instead of his. It is my opinion that women did not find Chucky particularly attractive, his mother being an extreme exception. He was not simply the apple of Aunt Lucy's eye but the whole basket of fruit.

The night before he was to leave for basic training, I stopped by his house to cheer him up. He lay sprawled on his bed staring morosely up at the ceiling. Chucky had about the greatest bedroom anyone could imagine, and it was outfitted with every truly great toy ever made. I will mention only one: an electric train that ran all the way around the walls on a shelf just above the windows and doors, with little towns, forests and mountains, farms with cows grazing in pastures, sidings and trestles and even tunnels, one of which ran through my heart. Even though he had long ago lost interest in it, Chucky never let me play with the train, giving the excuse that it was for my own good, because he would have to break my arm if he ever caught me touching it. To look upon that train, so close and yet so far, was pure torture. On the plus side, Chucky was going off to war the next day.

I did my best to cheer him up, but without much success. "It's just so unfair, Chucky, that you're the one who got drafted," I told him. "You don't even like war."

"Tell me about it!"

I sighed. "I sure wish it was me going instead of you."

"I wish it was you, too."

That surprised me. Usually, Chucky didn't seem to care all that much about what happened to me. "Thanks," I said. "I really do think you'll like the war, once you get used to it, Chucky. Just think, a few weeks from now you could be charging a machine-gun nest in Sicily or some other neat place."

"Would you just shut up and go home!"

"But you'll be a hero!"

"Don't bet on it!"

"Of course, it won't be all fun, Chucky," I pointed out. "The part I'd hate most would be having to take showers with a bunch of other naked guys. Man, just think of having to get naked around a couple monsters like the Scragg twins! Wheweee! The army should give medals for taking showers with the Scraggs!"

"Arrrrhhhh!" howled Chucky. "Showers with the Scraggs! I never even thought of that! I can't stand it! Arrrrhhhh!"

That's when Uncle Charles called to me from downstairs. "Patrick! Stop trying to cheer up Chucky and come down here!"

"Okay!" I called back. "Anyway, Chucky, I'll be at the train to see you off tomorrow morning."

"Arrrhhh!" cried Chucky. "Showers with the Scraggs!"

When I got downstairs, Uncle Charles frowned at me over the top his newspaper. "Good job," he said. "You really improved Chucky's mood."

"The least I could do," I said.

Uncle Charles was almost as fond of war as I was. Sometimes he and I would discuss the latest battles at great length. We'd sprawl out on his den floor to pore over maps of North Africa, Europe, and the South Pacific and try to keep track of all the different battlefields. I wasn't supposed to mention the war around Aunt Lucy, though. She had been in a funk—my mother's word—ever since Chucky's draft notice had arrived. On this particular evening she sat across the room from Uncle Charles, rocking furiously back and forth, which wouldn't have been too unusual if she had been in a rocking chair. I could tell she had been crying.

"I simply can't understand, Charles, why the draft board can't get it through its thick head that Chucky is too sensitive for war," she said, completely ignoring me. "Surely, you can pull some strings, Charles?"

"Lucy, we've been through this ten dozen times. I can't get Chucky classified Four-F because he's scared! Besides, the army will make a man out of him, you wait and see. It'll be good for him."

"It will, Aunt Lucy," I put in. "It really will. Chucky will love it, once he gets to shoot his rifle and throw grenades and starts doing neat stuff like bayonet practice and—"

"You stay out of this, you little warmonger!" Aunt Lucy snapped.

"Yeah, you're a big help, Patrick," Uncle Charles growled. "What would I do without you?"

I could see my opinion wasn't appreciated, so I stomped out the door and wandered off home.

The next morning I was up at dawn to see Chucky off on the train. That was something I wouldn't miss for the world. All of his aunts and uncles showed up to bid him farewell, along with about three hundred cousins, three grandparents, and one great-grandparent—old Marcus Winslow, one of the last of Teddy Roosevelt's Rough Riders.

Everyone cheered when Aunt Lucy and Uncle Charles drove up with Chucky in their spiffy black Hudson. It may have been jealousy on my part, but I got the impression Chucky had just been dragged by his heels out from under a bed. His clothes were ruffled and even buttoned wrong and his hair looked as if something had wintered in it. Uncle Charles smiled broadly at everyone, but he, too, seemed somewhat rumpled and out of sorts, as if maybe he had just dragged someone out from under a bed. Aunt Lucy looked a total wreck. At least she wasn't crying, but probably only because she had run dry. When it came time for Chucky to board the train, Uncle Charles practically had to use a tire iron to pry him out of Aunt Lucy's arms, although I wasn't certain who was clinging hardest to whom. Chucky seemed a little peeved at all the cheering, possibly because his many relatives seemed so happy to be sending him off to war. After boarding the train, he soon appeared at a window. He slumped into a seat and stared miserably out at the crowd of his well-wishers. Presently, two other inductees from Blight appeared at the window. Grinning broadly, one of them threw an arm around Chucky's neck and and the other gave him a friendly knuckle rub on his scalp. Great-grandpa Marcus pointed and shouted, "Why, lookee there, Lucy! Chucky's already got hisself some *compañeros*. You won't have to worry about him being lonely now!"

Aunt Lucy smiled feebly. "Yes," she said, waving her hanky at Chucky. "They do seem glad to see him."

Glad? I thought. Shoot, Lister and Bo Scragg couldn't be happier, having someone like Chucky to pass the time with.

After Chucky's departure, Aunt Lucy sank into an even deeper funk, a funk apparently without bottom. It appeared for a while that she might remain in the funk for the duration of the war, but then a weird series of events occurred.

A week or so after Chucky left for basic training, a Western Union messenger handed Lucy a telegram. It was from the army.

"Something's happened to Chucky!" Lucy cried. "They've already killed him!"

Charles snatched the telegram from her hand. It wasn't as bad as he had expected but bad enough. In essence, the telegram expressed the army's concerns as to why Chucky hadn't shown up for basic training. "Why, that little . . . ," Charles muttered, using one of his famous interrupted curses.

Lucy was now practically beside herself with grief. Nothing could convince her that the army hadn't done away with Chucky the moment he arrived. I tried to comfort her. "Maybe you would enjoy the sound of Chucky's train racing around the tracks upstairs," I suggested.

"Not a chance," she said.

A week or so after the telegram arrived, two FBI agents showed up at the Winslows' and asked Lucy if she had heard anything from Chucky. She practically went into hysterics, hopping up and down and screaming that the army had killed Chucky and that they should go ask the army what it had done with him, and did they think she was into psychic channeling with deceased persons, and so on. The agents were so shaken up by her reaction that they sat with her until she calmed down. They showed her such kindness and understanding that Lucy finally asked them if they would like some tea. That would be nice, they said. Pretty soon they were on a first-name basis. The agents' names were Bill and Jack, or something simple like that, and they were both formerly country boys from Utah. FBI Director J. Edgar Hoover himself had asked them to check into Chucky's disappearance, they said, or otherwise they wouldn't have bothered her.

When I heard the FBI had come looking for Chucky, I couldn't have been more proud of him. Here I had assumed Chucky would never amount to anything, as did most of his relatives, and now J. Edgar Hoover, the director of the FBI, had sent *two* agents out to look for him. If Mr. Hoover thought he was that important, to use up the valuable time of two of his agents, why, Chucky must have been up to something pretty darned important. Mr. Hoover certainly wouldn't waste two agents to track down Chucky simply because he failed to show up for basic training. Anyone who knew Chucky knew he'd be totally useless as a soldier anyway and that the army would be a whole lot better off without him, unless it suddenly needed someone to lead a retreat. Chucky would be good at that. Even Uncle Charles said so. I figured the FBI had to be after Chucky for some other reason, maybe some particular talent nobody even suspected him of possessing. It didn't matter now, though, because I figured Aunt Lucy was right. Chucky had to be dead. And soon I would have proof of it.

One day after finishing my paper route, I decided to stay in town that night and take in a movie: *Commandos Strike at Dawn*. It was wonderful, my kind of movie, but it made me think about Chucky, and how if he hadn't gotten killed, he'd have had a chance to be a hero or at least maybe get to do some neat stuff like the commandos in the film. Because I had to sit through the film twice to make sure I hadn't missed any detail, it was nearly eleven o'clock when I finally staggered out of the theater dazed and stiff. The streets were empty and silent and kind of creepy, with an eerie stillness hanging like a fog over the town. I decided my best bet for the night was to head out to Birchwood and slip into Uncle Charles's house for the night and sleep on the living room couch. It was only after I had pedaled all the way out to Birchwood that I remembered that Aunt Lucy had started locking the doors ever since Chucky had disappeared. Maybe she thought that if the army had murdered Chucky, it might sneak in and murder her and Uncle Charles next. I knew I could pound on the door until Uncle Charles came down and opened it, but then he would have to lecture me for half an hour and it wasn't worth the bother. Instead, I tried a few windows along the side of the house until I found one Lucy had forgotten to lock. Minutes later I was zonked out on the couch. Normally, I wouldn't have stirred again until Lucy started banging pots and pans out in the kitchen and yelling at me to get ready for breakfast. Scarcely had I settled into one of my favorite dreams, however, when something, a sudden chill, a stirring of air, something, nudged me awake. I rolled over on my back and shoved myself partway up on my elbows. Chucky's ghost was standing in the doorway of the kitchen, looking straight at me. Even in the dim glow cast through the window by an outside porch light, I could see every detail of his face, right down to his pouty lips and bad hair. The ghost seemed as startled by me as I was by it. For a second, I thought it was about to say something. Oddly, at that very moment something awakened Uncle Charles. He sprang out of bed and thundered down the hallway in his nightshirt, fumbling shells into his 12-gauge shotgun and shouting out some very bad words. My name popped up, a little island in a stream of profanity.

"Stop!" he shouted at me, as if I were the problem. "Stop that damn screeching, Patrick! What's wrong? Burglars? What? Speak!"

I told him what I'd seen, but he was too excited to comprehend it.

"Slow down!" he yelled. "Stop babbling! I can't understand a word you're saying!"

"Awsawanghostenkitchen," I explained, hoping he would calm down and stop waving the shotgun about.

"I'm standing right here, Patrick," he said. "You don't have to screech. Now what's this about a ghost?"

"I saw a ghost," I told him. "It was standing right there. It was about to speak to me. It was Chucky's ghost."

"Chucky's ghost?" Uncle Charles said, removing the shells from the shotgun. "First of all, Patrick, you were dreaming. Second, there's no such thing as ghosts. Third, Chucky isn't dead. No matter what Lucy thinks, he's hiding out somewhere. So he wouldn't have his ghost running around waking me up in the middle of the night, now would he?"

"What is it?" Aunt Lucy cried as she rushed up. "Is it the army?"

"No, it's not the army," Uncle Charles said. "It's nothing. Patrick was having a nightmare."

"I saw Chucky's ghost, Aunt Lucy," I attempted to explain.

"Chucky's ghost?" she said. "Hmmmm. Well, I'll go make us some hot cocoa. That will calm us all down, and maybe we'll still be able to get some sleep."

I for one didn't get any sleep the rest of the night. Shortly before dawn I thought I heard something on the stairs, but I had the good sense not to open my eyes. There are only so many ghosts a person can stand in one night. Later, though, I would do a lot of thinking about Chucky's ghost.

"I sure miss Chucky," I said to Aunt Lucy one day. "Everywhere I look, something reminds me of him. A few minutes ago, I was looking at his train and—"

"Not a chance," she said.

A couple of weeks later, I was finishing up my paper route when a car pulled up alongside of me. Bill and Jack, the FBI agents, got out.

"How you doing, Patrick?" Bill said.

"Fine," I said.

"We just happened to be in the neighborhood," Jack said. "Thought we might have a little visit with you, if that's okay."

"You bet," I said. It wasn't every day I got to visit with the FBI.

"You know, Patrick, we have talked with just about everybody who's ever known Chucky in his entire life, and there's not a soul has any idea where he could be hiding out. Now we know you're a sharp guy, get about town a lot, keep your eyes open, and we thought maybe a smart kid like you might have picked up a few clues. Any kind of a lead you can give us?"

"Well, I can tell you where you've gone wrong," I said. Right away I had their total attention.

"How's that?" Jack asked.

"You keep looking for Chucky to be hiding out somewhere, but he isn't. Chucky is dead."

"Dead?" said Bill.

"And how do you know that, Patrick?"

"I saw his ghost, that's how." If that didn't just about bowl both of them over right there in the street, I don't know what could have.

"You saw his ghost?" Jack said. "Where was this exactly."

"In my aunt Lucy's kitchen. I was sleeping on the couch and woke up all of a sudden and there was Chucky's ghost standing in the doorway to the kitchen. And then my uncle Charles came running down the hallway, making a terrible fuss, and when I looked again, the ghost was gone."

Jack and Bill seemed disappointed. "You sure you weren't dreaming?" Jack said.

"I know I wasn't dreaming," I said.

"Yeah, well," Bill said. "I guess we'd better be going. Thanks. Sorry to have bothered you."

"Anytime," I said. "Always glad to help out the FBI. Oh, wait a second, I just remembered something interesting."

"Like what?" Bill said, still moving toward the car.

"The ghost was eating a sandwich."

The agents stopped, looked at each other, then turned back toward me.

"A sandwich," Jack said.

"Yeah," I said. "A ham sandwich. A big slice of ham was sticking out the side of it. I could see it plain as day."

I could tell I had the agents' undivided attention, so I paused for a moment, to let the suspense build.

"Get on with it," Bill said.

"Now what I've been wondering is," I went on, "what kind of ham sandwich would a ghost eat? Would it be a real ham sandwich or would it be a ghost ham sandwich. If it was a ghost ham sandwich, that wouldn't be bad, but if it was a real ham sandwich, it would be kind of gross, because you would see it getting all chewed up and then going down into the ghost's stomach and . . ." I didn't finish. The agents were already in their car and half a block down the street, still accelerating.

The very next day the FBI raided Uncle Charles and Aunt Lucy's house and dragged Chucky down out of the attic.

"Chucky!" Aunt Lucy cried. "Thank goodness, you're alive!"

Bill and Jack were rather cross with Lucy but said they doubted she would have to go to jail for hiding Chucky. They said it was pretty obvious that Uncle Charles had no knowledge Chucky had been living in the attic the whole time. Chucky had never even left town. As the train pulled out of the station, he had shaken loose from the Scraggs and stepped off on the far side of the tracks.

Lucy was pretty upset until she heard that Chucky wouldn't be going off to war for a while.

"The army probably won't be too hard on him," Bill told Lucy. "Probably lock him up in the stockade for a while. Maybe the war will be over by the time he gets out."

"That would be nice," Aunt Lucy said. "He's way too sensitive for war, you know."

"Shucks, Lucy," Jack told her. "He'll even have some hometown boys to keep him company in the stockade. You happen to know the Scragg boys?"

Later, I asked Uncle Charles if he knew how the FBI agents figured out that Chucky had been hiding in the attic all along.

"They said somebody tipped them off," he said. "They wouldn't say who."

"Well, I'll be a . . . ," I said. "That dirty rotten, no-good . . . !"

Aunt Lucy seemed greatly relieved to have Chucky out of the attic. "It was such a worry," she told me. "He'd come down and wander around the house during the day while Charles was working, and he'd even sneak down for a snack in the middle of the night. I just knew sooner or later he'd get caught, if not by Charles then by somebody else. The informant really did both me and Chucky a great favor."

"Yes, it's all for the best, Aunt Lucy," I said. "Every cloud has a silver lining. So now that Chucky's gone, what do you think, can I mess with his train?"

"That silly old train. Mess with it all you want. Chucky will never know. Oh, the silliest thing, Patrick."

"What's that, Aunt Lucy?"

"The FBI agents said what gave Chucky away was a single clue—a ham sandwich!"

"Weird," I said.

"Yes! Why, what with the meat rationing for the war, we haven't had a speck of ham in the house for over a year! Isn't that the strangest thing? A ham sandwich!"

"I was wondering about Chucky's bow and arrow," I said. "I guess it would be all right if I used that, too, hunh, Aunt Lucy?"

"So Chucky was hiding in the attic all along," Devon said. "Was there a bathroom up there? I hope there was a bathroom. I never heard of an attic with a bathroom."

"I'm not up on all the technical details," I explained.

"The house is right there. We could go check and see if the attic has a bathroom, if you're not bothered by spiders and bats."

"I guess not," she said. "When does this story get to the bear, anyway?"

"Right now," I said.

Uncle Charles was in his office at the timber company one morning when he got a phone call from one of his logging-camp foremen:

"We got a problem up here, Mr. Winslow. The cook shot a sow bear the other night, because it kept trying to claw its way into the cook shack. Next morning some of the men happened by the bear's den and heard a cub crying and they brought it back into camp. We don't know what to do with it."

"Let me think about that, Buck," Uncle Charles said. "Okay, how about this? Conk it on the head!" He hung up the phone. He thought that was the end of it, but a short while later Buck showed up at the office. He pulled the tiny bear out of his jacket pocket and held it out to Uncle Charles. "I couldn't bring myself to conk it," he said. "None of the men would do it either. It's just too cute. So I figured I'd let you do it."

"And you call yourselves loggers," Uncle Charles said. "A bunch of girls is more like it. Give it to me, Buck."

The foreman handed over the cub and backed off, cringing slightly. Uncle Charles had a reputation for being a very hard man, and Buck said later he expected the cub to get conked right then and there. Instead, Charles cupped the bear in one hand and held it up to the light to examine it. "Why, its eyes aren't even open yet," he said. The cub made a crying sound.

"Sounds just like a human baby, don't it?" Buck said.

"Yeah," Charles said. "It is a cute little devil." He cleared his throat. "Now, Buck, this is probably something you don't know, but cute is one of nature's devices for preserving its young. It doesn't apply just to animals either. Many a dumb and useless human being has survived and prospered for no other reason than the good luck of being cute. My wife comes to mind. Not that I think Lucy is dumb and useless, mind you. What I'm saying is, she would never forgive me if she heard I did the sensible thing and disposed of something this cute. All I can do, if I want a minute's peace ever again, is to take the cub home and let Lucy deal with it. That's the only reason I don't conk it right now, you understand. So I guess you know what to tell the men about this."

"It's your wife's fault?"

"That's the way I see it, Buck."

A short while later, Uncle Charles walked into the kitchen at home and handed Lucy a paper sack. "Here's a little something for you."

Lucy was not the kind of person to get excited over a gift presented in a paper sack. "What is it?" she said wearily. She was back in her funk. The letters from Chucky complained bitterly about life in the stockade, particularly having to shower with the Scraggs. She had written to the officer in charge and explained how Chucky was so sensitive, and asked him to do something about the Scragg boys. The officer hadn't yet replied. She peered listlessly into the sack.

"A puppy?"

"Even worse," Uncle Charles said. "A baby bear."

"A baby bear!" cried Lucy, brightening. "Why, it is! A tiny bear! If it isn't the cutest thing in the world! Its eyes aren't even open yet! Do I get to keep it? Of course I do!"

Uncle Charles was pleased with himself. This was the first time in months he'd seen Lucy emerge from her funk. "Sure," he said. "It's all yours. Of course, you'll have to raise it until it's old enough to support itself out in the wilds."

"I'll call Ed Barnes right away and find out what to feed it," she said, referring to the local veterinarian. "I bet it's half starved."

Two hours later Lucy had the bear wrapped in a baby blanket and was feeding it out of a nursing bottle the vet had given her. The cub made tiny mewing sounds as it slurped away. Rocking to and fro in her rocker, Lucy couldn't take her eyes off the bear.

"Well, I've wasted enough time," Uncle Charles said. "Got to get back to the office. There's a war on, you know." He headed for the door.

"Let's see," Lucy murmured. "What shall I name it?"

Halfway out the door, Charles stopped, turned, and stared at his wife. "Name it? Lucy, I don't think it's a good idea to name a wild critter. The time might come when we might have to, uh, deal with it, uh, rather harshly. See, it's like naming a steer, for example. The time comes you have to slaughter it, there's a big difference between knocking off 'the steer' and knocking off 'Old Ned.'" See what I'm saying, Lucy? This little guy will weigh three hundred pounds or more before long, have claws like meat hooks, teeth the size of railroad spikes and—"

"Pooky," Lucy said. "I'll name him Pooky."

"Cute," Uncle Charles muttered, shaking his head. "It'll get you every time."

Lucy thought he was talking about the bear.

When Pooky's eyes popped open a week or so later, they focused first on his new mother, a slightly plumpish lady with tousled blonde hair and the wide blue eyes of a person who seems never quite to have understood the question, whatever the question might be.

By the first day of summer, Pooky was the size and shape of a basketball, a shiny black hairy basketball. In no time at all, Lucy had him housebroken and trained to respond to his name. Every day she baked him pancakes or biscuits to go with his basic dog food. He also ate leftover mash potatoes and gravy, macaroni and cheese, chicken and dumplings, tuna casserole, salmon loaf (one of his favorites), spaghetti, stew, peas, beans and spinach, and just about anything the

Winslows had left over from breakfast, lunch, and dinner. Lucy made sure plenty was left over. At the rate the bear was expanding in all directions, Uncle Charles said, he couldn't tell if Lucy was fattening him up with all the leftovers or inflating him with a tire pump. Still, Pooky seemed endlessly hungry. As soon as he had finished gobbling up his breakfast, he would go and sit by the refrigerator and cry like a baby, a sound that broke Lucy's heart.

"You'll never guess what Pooky did today," Lucy said to Uncle Charles one evening as he returned from work and flopped down in his favorite chair.

"I can hardly wait to hear," he said.

"He stood up on his hind feet and opened the refrigerator door by himself, just like a little man! Isn't that the cutest thing!"

Uncle Charles stared thoughtfully off into space. Presently he asked, "What's for supper?"

"You probably think it's some of those German sausages you had made up at Ye Olde Smokehouse yesterday, don't you? Well, it isn't. We're having baked beans on toast! Yum, doesn't that sound good?"

The next day Charles sent over a mechanic from the timber company shop. The mechanic put a latch on the refrigerator that the bear couldn't open. When Charles came home that evening, there were two refrigerators in the kitchen. "I bought one just for Pooky," Lucy explained. "I thought it would be nice if he had his own refrigerator. That way he can get a snack whenever he wants. Don't you think that is so cute?"

Uncle Charles stared silently at the refrigerator for a long moment. When he finally spoke, his voice was strained, raspy. "Next week I'm going to take Pooky out into the woods. Teach him how to tear apart rotted logs. Find grubs and bugs. And eat them. Like a real bear."

"Oh, Charles, don't be crude," Lucy said. "You know how I hate it."

The following Saturday, Uncle Charles fastened a thick

leather collar around Pooky's neck and attached a chain to it. He dragged the cub skidding and whining out to the pickup truck, boosted it up into the cab, and slammed the door. Pooky clearly suspected something. Uncle Charles got in the cab and started the motor. The cub looked around frantically for a means of escape. It saw Lucy out in the yard, waving.

"Good-bye, Pooky!" Lucy called. "Have a nice day!"

"Maawmaaw!" cried Pooky, flattening himself against the window. "Maawmaw!"

Uncle Charles almost ran into a birch tree. He said later the bear's cry sent a chill up his spine. He said he knew at that moment that Pooky was going to be more trouble than he or anyone else had ever even imagined.

The outing was unsuccessful. As Uncle Charles said, you can never find a rotten log when you need one. He spent most of the morning dragging the bear through the woods and at last he found a log sufficiently decayed that he could kick it apart. It contained a rather nice helping of grubs. The bear sniffed the grubs, then looked quizzically up at Charles.

"Grubs don't taste as bad as you might think," Charles told Lucy that evening. "I think Pooky might have eaten some himself, if they'd come with gravy and a side of bacon."

By the time the first snow fell in November, Charles thought it was time for Pooky to start hibernating, just like a regular bear. "If he's hibernating, you won't have to worry about him feeding himself," he told Lucy. "He's got enough fat to last him the next three years. So I'm going to take him out to the den he was found in and stuff him into it. Next spring he'll wake up with a fine appetite and he'll darn sure figure out how to find some regular bear food."

"You'll do nothing of the sort," Lucy said. "Pooky can hibernate right here. I've already fixed him up a nice little cave in the attic. We'll leave a window cracked so he gets lots of fresh air."

Locked in the attic, Pooky cried for three days straight and nearly broke Lucy's heart. Finally, he crawled into the cave and went to sleep. The winter passed so peacefully Uncle Charles sometimes even forgot that he had a bear in the attic.

The next time Uncle Charles heard from Pooky was on April Fools' Day. As always, the cry sent a chill up his spine. "Maawmaaw! Maawmaaaaaa!" He couldn't be sure, but now he thought the cry was deeper, more mature, maybe even a bit threatening. He shuddered and went off to work.

When Charles returned that evening, Pooky was sitting in his favorite chair. "Get out of my chair!" he ordered. The bear gave him a blank look, faking incomprehension, or so Charles suspected. When Pooky refused to move, Charles tried to drag him out of the chair, but the bear dug his claws into the leather and cried out, "Maawmaaw! Maawmaaaaa!"

Lucy came out of the kitchen. "Charles, stop that! Don't play so rough! Can't you see you're upsetting Pooky?"

"He's in my chair and I want him out of it!"

"Pshaw! There are other chairs, Charles! Why make a fuss over that old thing? Now, for heaven's sake, stop antagonizing the little bear." She walked back in the kitchen.

Charles flopped down in a chair across the room from Pooky. The bear appeared to be grinning at him. It was leaner now, already maturing from cub into yearling, the bear equivalent of a teenager. The thought brought Chucky to mind. Now that was scary: a bear version of Chucky.

"Any word from Chucky today?" he called out to Lucy.

"Who?"

"Chucky. Your son."

"Oh, right. No, nothing from him."

The bear grinned at Charles.

As spring turned into summer, Pooky lengthened out and became leaner still, despite the twenty-pound bags of dog food Lucy poured into him. Powerful muscles could now be seen rippling under the shaggy fur as he padded out to the kitchen to check his refrigerator, his claws clicking ominously on the hardwood floors. The steady stream of visitors that once found the little Pooky so cute and amusing gradually diminished to a dribble and then stopped altogether.

I was once sitting in Lucy's kitchen with Great-grandfather Marcus Winslow, listening to him tell stories about his days as a Rough Rider with Teddy Roosevelt. He lived with my aunt Dierdra, who had dropped him off for the afternoon while she went shopping. I assumed that he knew about Pooky.

"So there we was, moving up San Juan Hill, when Teddy says to me, Marcus, that's what he called me, Marcus, Marcus he says, you take some of the boys and—" At that moment Pooky walked in, stood up on his hind feet, opened his refrigerator door, studied the contents, finally selected one of the lunch sacks, grabbed it in his teeth, and walked out.

"What did Teddy want you to do?" I asked.

Grampa Marcus stared after the bear.

"Teddy Roosevelt," I prompted. "You were going up San Juan Hill, remember, Grampa?"

"Did you just now notice something kind of peculiar?" he asked.

"No," I said, for it was commonplace for Pooky to stroll out and get a snack out of the refrigerator. "Why?"

"No reason. Forget I mentioned it. So anyway Teddy he says to me . . ."

More than one old person was startled by the sight of Pooky. Daffy old Mrs. Swisher lived several miles out in the country and each Sunday drove by the Winslow house on her way to church. Sometimes she drove by on Saturday or even Friday, thinking it was Sunday. One such Saturday Uncle Charles was sprawled out on the living room couch wearing only his shorts. He was reading the newspaper and smoking a cigar. Normally, he wasn't allowed to smoke cigars in the house, but Lucy was away somewhere for several days. It is the opinion of some members of the family that Pooky may have thought Charles was on fire, when he saw him blow smoke out of his mouth. The bear got out of his chair and walked over to Charles to study him more closely. Charles and the bear stared at each other at close range for a moment, and then Charles blew a puff of smoke into the bear's face and told him to get away. Pooky sat down on his haunches and studied Charles even more intently, apparently trying to get to the bottom of the mystery. Charles blew more smoke in his face. The bear inhaled it. He seemed to enjoy it, the first admirable quality Uncle Charles said he had detected in the bear. Then he made the mistake of setting the cigar in an ashtray while he turned a page of the newspaper. In a flash, Pooky snatched up the cigar and raced out of the house.

"Come back here you little . . . !" Charles yelled in one of his interrupted curses. "You've stolen my food, my attic, my favorite chair, and the affections of my wife, but you're not going to steal my cigars!" It's unlikely that Uncle Charles yelled that exact sentence at the time of the incident but instead worked it out over a period of several days before relating the event to some his friends. In any case there is reliable historic testimony that the bear raced out of the house with the cigar and shot up a slender birch tree next to the house. Under his weight, the birch swayed out over the house and the bear dropped down onto the roof. He then walked up to the ridge and sat his rear end down on the edge of the chimney. It was at that moment that Mrs. Swisher drove by.

Always quick to notice any suspicious activity on the part of her neighbors, in case they happened to be spies or saboteurs, Mrs. Swisher stopped by the sheriff's office and gave him a report.

"Let me get this straight," the sheriff said. "You saw Winslow out in his front yard wearing only his shorts. He was shaking his fist and swearing a blue streak."

"That's right, Sheriff."

"And there was a bear up on the roof?"

"Yes."

"The bear was sitting on the chimney?"

"Yes. He looked like a hairy little man, with his hands resting on his knees, just sitting there gazing out over the countryside, he was. It *could* have been a hairy little man, I suppose, but I'm pretty sure it was a bear."

"And the bear was smoking a cigar?"

Mrs. Swisher gave an affirmative nod. "So what do you think, Sheriff?"

The sheriff neglected to mention in his notes what he thought, but because he regarded our entire family with considerable suspicion it is likely he found Mrs. Swisher's story to be a credible account by an objective witness of a fairly routine occurrence.

Uncle Charles waited until the first huckleberries ripened in early July and then he hauled Pooky back out to his old den in the mountains. He slipped the collar off Pooky's head and while the bear happily gorged himself on huckleberries, Charles got in his truck and drove off. He spent the rest of the day fishing up Pack River. When he returned to the den in the evening, the huckleberry patch had been stripped bare of berries and there was no sign of Pooky. Uncle Charles smiled all the way home.

"I suppose it's just as well," Aunt Lucy said. "You just never know. Sooner or later he might have become a nuisance."

One evening in November, Charles and Lucy were seated in their living room, he in his favorite chair, reading the newspaper and listening to the radio, she in her rocker, knitting. "It's supposed to snow again tonight," he said.

"I'm not surprised," Lucy said. "It's turning awfully cold."

Charles studied her. "I guess you're not worried about Pooky then."

"Oh no," she said. "I'm sure he'll be all right. Bears know how to survive in cold weather."

"He's hibernating in the attic again, isn't he?" Uncle Charles said.

"How did you know?"

"Tracks in the backyard."

"He showed up at the door the other day, and I couldn't say no," Lucy said. "He's gotten awfully big. And his breath is terrible. He's not the least bit friendly, either."

"He'll be a lot less friendly when he wakes up in the spring," Charles said. "Bears have notoriously bad tempers when they come out of hibernation."

"He's not cute anymore, either," Lucy said. "You should do something about him, Charles."

Charles regarded her thoughtfully for several moments but did not respond.

Pooky woke up on the dot of April Fools' Day, just as he had the year before. He was, as Charles had predicted, in a very bad temper, with a raging appetite for something more substantial than dog food. Lucy and Charles hid in the bathroom until he was gone. A poodle, a Doberman pinscher, two cats, and a pet goat were later reported missing from the neighborhood.

"Why, that miserable, no-good . . . !" said Uncle Charles.

Pooky would be a full-size adult bear come the following November. Maybe, Charles thought, he'll find himself a normal den, a regular bear's den, even though a regular bear's den doesn't have insulated walls, central heating, and free snacks in the refrigerator. So he wasn't greatly surprised when the day after the first snowfall the next November, he and Lucy heard something come thumping up the back porch and bang against the door.

"Don't answer it!" cried Lucy. "I know it's him."

"Maybe not," Charles said. "It could be the wind."

Then came a deep, rough, rumbling voice: *MAAW-MAAAAW! MAAWMAAWWW!*

"Holy . . . !" said Uncle Charles.

Pooky was so big he could barely squeeze through the opening into the attic.

Uncle Charles and Aunt Lucy lay awake all that night, staring up at the ceiling, through which they could hear the hard clicking sounds of Pooky's claws as he paced back and forth. Then they heard him grunting as he squeezed back down through the attic opening. He soon appeared at the bedroom door, looking from one to the other of them. Lucy thought she saw him lick his chops. She pointed a finger at herself. "Maawmaawww!" she said. "Maawmaawww!"

Charles thought it rather inconsiderate of Lucy.

Presently, the bear padded down to its refrigerator, which Lucy had had to the good sense to stock with horse meat. Fully sated, Pooky returned to the attic, pausing only for a thoughtful moment before the door of the bedroom.

"You know Pooky's going to be totally lethal when he comes out of hibernation next April," Charles said.

"I know," Lucy said. "I think you should sneak up and shoot him while he's asleep, Charles."

"I'm not shooting anything named Pooky," Charles said. "I've got a better solution."

In January, Charles and Lucy moved to Tucson. Lucy wrote to Chucky to tell him the house was his, whenever he got out of the army. She warned him about the bear in the attic. Chucky in the meantime had been released from the stockade in time to distinguish himself in some of the fiercest battles of Europe. He often joked that combat was a piece of cake, after being locked up for a year with the Scragg brothers.

Chucky was surprised and pleased to learn the house was his, but he had no plans to return to Idaho anytime soon. He did manage to find a couple of renters, though.

"I don't get it," Lister Scragg said to his brother Bo as they prepared to turn in on their first night at the house. "Man, after all the fun we had with Chucky, he still rents us this palace for a measly twenty-five bucks a month. He must be nuts."

"Yeah, well, his old lady and his old man weren't like the sanest people in the world. I mean, take those two refrigerators in the kitchen. And the freezer is crammed full of beef steak! What kinda deal is that? And they left all this furniture and even a couple boxes of cigars. It's crazy, man."

"Maybe it's some kinda joke," Lister said.

"You suppose?" Bo said. "After all, tomorrow's April Fools' Day, ain't it?"

Chucky wasn't too surprised when the Scraggs started missing their rent payments. He asked some friends to check around, but the Scraggs had suddenly and completely disappeared, never to be heard from again.

The house remained empty over the spring and summer, but that fall there was a small but mysterious fire in the attic. The fire chief said it looked as if somebody had been trying to light cigars with kitchen matches. Probably some kids fooling around, he speculated.

Abandoned, the house eventually fell victim to time and the weather. No one ever lived there again, although every November when the weather turned cold and the snow began creeping down the mountains, daffy old Mrs. Swisher would stop by the sheriff's office with reports of her weird sightings:

"I tell you, Sheriff, I'm not imagining this. I've seen it peering out of that little upstairs window every fall about this time. You go check it out right now, Sheriff, and you'll see I'm right. There's a bear in the attic!"

Not being stupid, the sheriff never did check it out.

"What?" cried Devon. "The bear ate the Scraggs? Are you telling me Pooky ate the Scraggs? Gross! Gag!"

"Did I say that? Did I say Pooky ate the Scraggs? I did not! Now, here's your house. You better not tell your grandmother I said the bear ate the Scraggs, because I didn't. Otherwise, no more visits to the library with me."

She got out and stomped off toward her house.

"Wait!" I yelled after her. "You forgot Teddy! You forgot your cute little teddy bear!"

She went in the house and slammed the door. Women! I'll never understand them, not even the little ones.

The Magic Tree

"Flynn's back," my mother said at supper that evening.

"Uncle Flynn's back?" I exclaimed. "Neato!"

My life was definitely looking up. Not only had I just been sprung from seventh grade for three whole weeks of Christmas vacation, but one of my two most favorite people in the entire world had suddenly returned to our little logging town of Blight, Idaho. Uncle Flynn, in fact, was one of two men in my life whom I had under serious consideration as role models for myself. The other was the odiferous old woodsman Rancid Crabtree, who had never worked a day in his life and spent all of his time fishing and hunting. He drank homemade whiskey, chewed and spit tobacco, told outrageous lies, and never took baths except by accident and, in general, spent most of his life doing exactly as he pleased. For a role model, you just about couldn't do better than that. On the other hand, there was my uncle Flynn. Although pretty much Rancid's opposite, Uncle Flynn was definitely a contender as a role model.

"Yes, Flynn's back in town," Mom went on. "That worthless bum of a brother of mine is no doubt on the run again. He's holed up in the Blight Hotel with some skinny blonde broa . . . woman."

"Huh! No kidding! So Uncle Flynn got married! I wonder how come he never wrote and told me he got married?"

"Shut up and eat your gruel."

The neat thing about Uncle Flynn was that he made his living gambling. He won a lot of money at it, too, and always wore these really classy clothes and shiny black shoes, and smoked fat cigars and drove big cars and always seemed to have beautiful girlfriends and . . . Well, I tell you, at age twelve I found it pretty darn hard to choose between my smelly old friend Rancid and the dashing Flynn for a proper role model.

"Oh, I almost forgot," Mom said, looking up from her gruel. "Rancid stopped by earlier. He said he's going to drive up into the mountains tomorrow and thought you might enjoy going along."

"Why, yeah," I said. Could my luck get any better than this? Christmas vacation! Uncle Flynn back in town! And now an invitation from Rancid to go tramping about in the mountains with him! If it wasn't too much, it certainly was more than enough.

"Rancid said bring an ax," Mom added as an afterthought.

"An ax!" This was getting better all the time. We obviously would be doing some serious woodcraft.

"Yes," Mom said. "And he said for you to show up at the crack of dawn or he'd leave without you."

In the lingering dark of early morning I plodded through the snowy woods and arrived at Rancid's shack right on the dot of dawn. I knocked. No answer. Worried that he might have left without me, I pushed open the door and looked in. He was still in his bunk, snoring lustily.

"Rancid!" I yelled in disgust.

He popped bolt upright. "Gol-dang in tarnation! You! What you mean, startlin' a feller half to death?"

"I came right when you told me, the crack of dawn. Look out your window."

"Wahl, Ah'll be danged, the crack of dawn. So thet's what it looks like. Ah've heard folks mention it but—"

"And you're not even dressed!"

"Ah shore is!" He threw off the covers and stepped out of the bunk, fully attired right down to his boots. I had forgotten that Rancid considered it a nuisance to take clothes off at night just to put them back on again in the morning. There was a lot of wisdom in that old man.

A half hour later we were well up into the mountains, bouncing along in Rancid's old heaterless truck.

"How much farther, Rance?" I asked, blowing on my frozen fingers.

"We're thar," he said, using a snowbank for a brake.

"But there's nothing here," I said. "Just that hillside covered with puny little fir trees."

"Them ain't puny fir trees, boy, them is Crimmas trees! Ah'm goin' into the Crimmas tree bidness."

"The Christmas tree business? Exactly where do I fit into to your Christmas tree business?"

"Git yer ax and foller me."

By sunset we had the truck stacked high with Christmas trees, several of which Rancid had cut himself.

"Wahl, Ah guess thet's enough. Ah'm plumb tuckered out from all thet wor . . . wor . . . choppin'. Now stop staggerin' around like thet and throw them last two trees on the truck. Why, wait a durn second! Would you look at thet!" He pointed at a scraggly, twisted little tree illuminated against the gathering gloom of night by a single ray of sunlight.

"So?" I said. "It's just a scrawny little old tree. Nobody's gonna buy that for a Christmas tree."

"Don't you be so shore, smarty. Thet's a magic tree."

"A magic tree?"

"Yep. Now you go cut it and we'll head fer home."

I slogged over to the little tree, whacked it off with one swing of the ax, and threw it up on the truck.

"I don't see why you call it a magic tree," I told Rancid as the old truck growled back down the mountain.

"Ah'll tell you why. Because it brangs the feller what owns it good luck! And Ah'll tell you what. All the money Ah makes offen thet magic tree, Ah gonna give it to you fer helpin' me out today."

"You mean all I get for slaving away all day cutting trees is the money you get from that miserable tree!"

"Yep, thet's part of its magic. Har! See, already it's brangin' me luck."

Rancid set up his Christmas tree business on an empty lot next to Grogan's War Surplus and across the street from the Blight Hotel. Sales were brisk, mostly because Rancid knew his market—poor but lazy people who didn't want to go up in the mountains and cut their own trees. He sold his trees for thirty-five cents apiece.

As with any vacation, time sped by. Three days before Christmas I felt a little depressed because I didn't have any money to buy presents for the family but even more depressed that the family didn't have money to buy presents for me. The only thing I had to count on was Rancid's magic tree. And what would that bring me? Five cents, tops. To cheer myself up I decided to stop in and visit Uncle Flynn in his tiny hotel room.

"Hi, kid," Uncle Flynn said, sitting cross-legged on the bed. "Pull up a wall and lean against it." He was playing solitaire on the side of a suitcase. His new wife, Flossy, said "Hi," then went back to peering out the window. "Now he's only got two trees left," she said. "Gee, I haven't had a Christmas tree since I was a kid."

Uncle Flynn laid out his cards for a new game of solitaire. "That's Flossy's entertainment," he said. "Watching old Crabtree sell his Christmas trees."

"You know what, Flynn," Flossy said. "You could go buy one of that old man's last two trees. We could put it up in the room and cut out little strips of paper and paste them into loops and make paper chains to decorate it. We could glue the strips together with fingernail polish. It'd be fun."

"Shhh! Listen!" Uncle Flynn said, putting a finger to his lips and a cupped hand to his ear.

"What is it?" Flossy whispered back.

"I think I just heard a crazy woman. She said she wanted to put up a Christmas tree in a hotel room."

Flossy called him a really bad name. I didn't think ladies even knew that name. Shoot, I'd just learned it myself. Uncle Flynn chuckled and went back to his cards.

"Oh no," Flossy said, glancing back out the window. "There goes another one. Darn! Now he's only got one left." She turned back from the window. Tears made shiny little streaks down her cheeks.

"Oh for cripes sake, Floss," Uncle Flynn said. "Are you cry-ing over a lousy tree? Don't cry! Stop it! I can't stand crying! Okay, okay, I'll buy a tree."

He jumped up from the bed and grabbed his overcoat. "C'mon, kid. You can help me haul that blasted tree up to the room."

Twenty minutes later Uncle Flynn and I dragged a scraggly little tree across the street and into the hotel lobby. Milo, the new desk clerk, looked startled. "Oh, no, no, no, Mr. Smith, you can't bring that awful tree in here. This is a hotel."

"It's a Christmas tree, Milo," Uncle Flynn said. "Are you by any chance insulting my Christmas tree?"

It was a tone of voice I'd never heard Uncle Flynn use before. Apparently Milo had, though. "Sorry," he said. "I guess it's all right, a Christmas tree. In a hotel room. What the heck."

Flossy was thrilled with the tree, but Uncle Flynn was grumpier than ever. "That miserable old Rancid Crabtree robbed me of five bucks for this scrawny excuse for a tree. Claimed it was some kind of magic tree, the old reprobate!"

"It's not scrawny, it's beautiful!" Flossy said. "It's magic to me, Flynn, you darling man."

"Five bucks?" I said.

I helped Uncle Flynn get the tree propped up in a corner and then headed for the door.

"Where you think you're going?" Uncle Flynn said.

"Got to catch Rancid," I said.

"Oh no, you don't," Uncle Flynn said. "You're gonna stay here and help Flossy make paper chains."

"Oh do, please," said Flossy. "It'll be fun."

I glanced out the window. Rancid was scurrying off. That was all right. I'd catch him at his cabin. "Okay," I said.

By the time Flossy and I got finished with it, the tree looked pretty nice. Even Uncle Flynn said so.

"Funny thing," he said, grinning at the tree. "It makes me laugh every time I look at it."

"Me, too," Flossy said. "We just got caught up in the Christmas spirit."

"Yeah, well, I sure got caught up in something," Uncle Flynn said. "My fingers are all stuck together from the nail polish on those stupid paper chains. If it don't come off, you're in big trouble, Floss."

As I started to leave, Uncle Flynn said, "You know, kid, it's not a good idea for me to be showing my face out on the street for a while, kind of a little misunderstanding I got with some guys. Anyway, I won't be doing much shopping this year. So here's something for you and the family." He handed me a rumpled wad of cash. "Get everybody something nice. If I hear you spent it all on yourself, I'll bust your kneecaps. Oh yeah, and thanks for your help with the, uh, so-called magic tree."

Flossy came over and gave me a kiss on the cheek. My feet lifted off the floor, and I floated out of the room and down

the stairs to the lobby. As I touched down on the faded car-
pet, I noticed two men in long black overcoats talking to the
desk clerk.

"Sounds kind of like you're looking for Mr. Smith," Milo
was telling them. "A neat little mustache, slicked-back hair.
Got a daffy blonde with him."

"A daffy blonde," one of the men said. "Sounds like our old
pal all right. I guess we'll just drop in and surprise him."

One of the men shoved past me and started up the stairs.

"Yeah," Milo went on. "Your pal is quite the guy. Can you
believe he put up a Christmas tree in his room, in a hotel
room? You ever hear of such a thing?"

"A Christmas tree?" the man at the desk said. "He put up a
Christmas tree in his hotel room?"

"Yeah, he really did," said Milo, giggling. "A Christmas
tree! Can you believe it?"

"Hey, Lou!" the man at the desk called to his associate on
the stairs. "Forget it. This ain't him."

I felt kind of sorry for the men because they obviously
were upset at not finding their pal. As they drove off, I sauntered out of the hotel and across the street, headed for Grogan's War Surplus. What better place to do a little Christmas
shopping? When I glanced at the vacant lot, now empty of
Christmas trees, I figured maybe I'd just let Rancid keep the
five dollars as a Christmas present. Might just as well,
because he probably wouldn't give it up anyway. I had to
smile, though, when I thought about it, how the cagey old
woodsman had put one over on Uncle Flynn, the master gam-
bler. Magic tree indeed! What a laugh.

'38 Pickup

O f all the firsts of a person's life, one that usually takes place sometime in the teenage years stands out above all others. It is the one that changes your life and introduces you to an experience more grand and wonderful, and scarier, too, than you had ever even imagined. Oh, it is a fearful and glorious and momentous occasion, that day you get your first driver's license. At least it was so for me.

I remember with crystalline clarity every little nuance of that steamy August day. For weeks I had practiced parallel parking the family car between two bales of hay in the field next to our farmhouse. Nevertheless, the very thought of having my parallel parking put to the test had turned me into a nervous wreck, if for no other reason than the rarity of finding a parking space between two bales of hay.

I memorized the entire booklet of driving rules, not a great accomplishment, because there were a lot fewer rules in those days. Mostly, you had to make sure you knew the hand signals for turning left and right and braking. Hand signals were important, because most cars didn't have turn signals and some didn't have brakes, at least any that worked all that well. What the hand signal for braking warned was, "I'm braking now but don't expect the car actually to stop." You also had to show you recognized the shapes of highway signs. Knowing the shape of the STOP sign was most important, particularly if you couldn't read the word "STOP" and were color blind. The frightening part of the experience, though, was demonstrating you knew how to drive to the satisfaction of the much-feared Driver's License Inquisitor. If I failed parallel parking, I'd probably be afoot the rest of my life. Night after night I lay awake worrying about the ordeal that loomed ahead, parallel parking in the infernal driving test!

The driver's license office wasn't too busy the day I turned up for my examination. The Inquisitor, a large, beefy man in cowboy boots, was leaning back in his chair with his feet propped on his bare desk. He was reading the newspaper and smoking a cigar. He looked over the top of the newspaper at me. He did not seem pleased at the interruption.

"I'm here for my driver's license exam," I said, my voice quaking only slightly.

"Why else would you show up on a day like this?" the Inquisitor growled. "Well, here's the written test." He shoved a little booklet at me.

I finished the written test and handed it in. The Inquisitor speed-read it in one second. "You passed," he said. "Congratulations. Now I suppose I have to take you out and see if you actually know how to drive a car."

Heaving a monstrous sigh and himself from the chair, he mopped the glistening sweat from his face with a huge red bandanna. Then he lumbered off down the hall toward the parking lot, with me following nervously and respectfully behind. I didn't want to do anything that would annoy the Inquisitor more than my mere existence already had. Suddenly, he stopped, turned, frowned, looked me up and down, and said, "Ah, hell, son, you know how to drive." Then he plodded back to his office and issued me my very first driver's license. The long, dreaded ordeal had turned out to be much easier than I'd ever imagined.

"Thank you very much, sir," I told the Inquisitor, greatly relieved. "This is a very important day for me and I much appreciate your expediting the whole process. I will endeavor to obey all the rules and work constantly to perfect my driving skills and—"

"Beat it," he said.

My mother was waiting for me outside in the car. "I passed!" I told her. "Scoot over. I'll drive."

While I waited for her laughter to subside, I began to get a sense that my prospects for tooling around in the family car were not such that I should hold my breath. "Well, at least by this fall I should be able to drive the car up in the mountains to go hunting," I said.

"Oh! Oh! Please stop!" Mom cried out. "You're making my sides ache!"

The odds of my acquiring the car as a hunting vehicle by fall did not appear any better than the odds of my tooling.

As I've often pointed out, the very best kind of hunting vehicle is any kind of vehicle belonging to somebody else: "Wow, Fred, that was one rough patch there. You wiped out your front bumper and tore off one of your doors. Anyway, as I was saying, the farmer turns to the traveling salesman and . . ." It's possible that I developed this theory about best hunting vehicles from my very first such vehicle.

A week or so after getting my license, I was helping a farmer repair his fence. He was called Freaky, although there was nothing at all odd about him except a name that sounded something like "freaky." I told Freaky of my sad plight, namely that even though I now had my driver's license, I would still have to two-wheel it out to my hunting grounds on my bike.

A kindly but famously tightfisted man, Freaky sympathized

with me. "You know what," he said. "Because you're such a good-hearted lad to be out here helping me repair this fence, I might just do you a little favor."

"I thought you were paying me," I said.

"No," he said. "Your mother loaned you to me. But about the favor. I got this old thirty-eight pickup truck and you can borrow it to go hunting. All you need do is make sure the gas tank is full when you return it."

"Wow, that's great, Freaky!" I said. "How can I ever repay you?"

"Well, if you insist," he said, "you can haul those four thousand bales of hay out of the field and stack them in the barn."

"I wasn't insisting," I said.

"It was worth a try," Freaky said.

That really surprised me. Decent though he was, it was so unlike Freaky, as far as I knew, to give something for nothing. The only possible answer was, I had charmed him into it with the warmth and sparkle of my personality.

When I told Mom the good news, a sadness seemed to come over her.

"Don't worry, Mom," I said. "I'll be real careful with the truck."

"It's not that," she said. "It's Freaky. I hadn't realized he'd lost his mind."

Freaky was as good as his word. When hunting season rolled around, the truck was practically mine. He even told me I could keep it at my place. It was a powerful 1938 Studebaker half-ton pickup, a two-wheel drive but with a first gear so low that truck could almost climb trees, and occasionally made the attempt. The truck was practically indestructible, at least much more so than I. Once having whacked my head soundly on a steel ceiling beam, I came up with a really zany idea: belts that would hold a person down on the seat and keep him from ricocheting about in the cab.

Now that I had wheels, four instead of the usual two, my hunting took on a whole new aspect. By getting up at four in the morning, I could drive out to my favorite mountain, hunt for an hour or so, and still be back in time for school, not that that was high on my list of priorities. Soon, desperate to get my first deer, I was hunting four and five days a week, but with no more success than when I'd hunted only on weekends with my bike.

One morning toward the end of deer season, I was sure I finally had my buck. My practice was to park the truck at the bottom of the mountain and then walk up an old skid trail in the dark to get in a good position before daylight. A thick, noisy crust had formed on the snow, but I could walk quietly by following my tracks of the day before. I knew a big whitetail buck hung out on that side of the mountain, and on this dark and icy morning I sensed he and I were about to converge.

As I worked my way up the skid trail, I suddenly heard a loud, startled snort from behind a patch of brush a dozen yards away. I froze, which wasn't too difficult because I was already half frozen. It was a good hour yet before it would be light enough to shoot, but the deer hadn't spooked. I knew he would have to make a terrible ruckus if he crashed off through the crusted snow, and I'd heard nothing after that single snort. I figured maybe he was having a bad dream. And I was it! Silent minute after silent minute slipped by. Scarcely breathing, I continued to freeze there on the snow-covered road. Numbness crept up my legs and bit by bit engulfed the entire lower half of my body. I sensed that major and valued portions of my anatomy were about to suffer frostbite. I breathed on my trigger finger to keep it limber. If only one part of me worked when dawn at last cracked, I wanted it to be that finger. Slowly the darkness faded from the land. I waited for a clear view of the buck's only possible route of escape. Stiff with cold, I moved like a frosted Frankenstein's monster toward the concealing patch of brush, my frozen pants crackling at every step. Still, the buck didn't run. Closer and closer I crept, but still he didn't run. He never ran! The patch of brush was empty. Why hadn't I heard him bound off through the crusted snow? Because he hadn't bounded. He had slipped away by carefully stepping in his own previous tracks!

I did not brag to my friends about this little adventure. My being outwitted by a simple-minded ruminant was something I did not wish to share with them. Most of my other hunts in the year that Freaky loaned me his pickup were not nearly so successful.

By the end of deer season I had practically come to think of the pickup as my own, but I was by no means stingy with it. Sometimes I would even let Freaky borrow his truck, if he had some real need for it, of course. Much to my surprise, he had turned out to be such a generous and kindly man, I certainly owed him some consideration. After all, he had furnished me the means not only of transporting myself into the mountains but into a realm of myself I had not yet explored, a place you can get to only under the power of your first driver's license and a vehicle that, no matter its condition, at least moves. Still, it seemed odd, when I thought about it. Why would a farmer turn over his old truck to a kid he scarcely knew and want nothing in return? Maybe he wasn't all that sane.

I also noticed my mother's sanity to be showing some slippage. She'd always done odd things, but this was odder than most. The very next summer she let Freaky graze his cows on our lower pasture. And she never charged him a dime. Irrational behavior in a neighbor is one thing, but when you see it in your own mother, it can make you pretty darn nervous.

Skinny in Traffic

Driving down to a business meeting the other day, I got held up in traffic while a city road crew installed some potholes. Potholes were my guess anyway, based on the evidence of previous road repairs.

I was already late for the meeting and growing increasingly agitated. I drummed my fingers on the steering wheel as I glanced around at my fellow detainees: an intense lady in a suit with a bow at her neck and a cigarette at her lips; a guy yelling into a cell phone in one hand while tugging his tie loose with the other; a young couple in heated discussion, no doubt about which of them would get the condo. I felt as if I'd been sucked into a universal one-star day.

And then I saw him. He was a couple of lanes over, calmly puffing a pipe, a skinny guy in a weathered hat and a week's growth of grizzled beard. His half-ton pickup truck, which didn't appear much younger than its owner, had a faded slide-in camper on behind and a battered aluminum boat in tow. The outboard motor was equally ancient, but somehow I knew that one brisk jerk on its starter cord would bring it purring to life. The whole outfit looked so . . . so . . . well, so *really neat*!

The skinny guy irritated the hell out of me. He was going fishing, and I was going to a meeting with my attorney. Was that fair?

Even though I'd never seen this particular guy before, I knew him well. For example, I knew if you asked him, "Got a knife on ya?" he'd reach into his pocket and haul out a little bone-handled jackknife. "Don't cut yerself," he'd say. "It's sharp." And of course it would be sharp, half the metal in the blade honed away over the past twenty years to keep it that way. He would be a man who kept a jackknife for twenty years. I'm a man who keeps a jackknife for twenty seconds: "Hey, where's my knife? I had it right here twenty seconds ago!"

I knew that here was a man who tied his own flies, loaded his own shells, smoked his own fish, cured his own jerky, cut his own firewood, sharpened his own jackknife. (Really, who has time nowadays to sharpen a jackknife?) He knew when the morel mushrooms pop up in the spring and the shaggy-manes in the fall, where the huckleberries grow like clusters of grapes, and when the elderberries are just right for wine.

Somewhere up in the mountains Skinny and his buddies, Fats and Virgil, have a secret place where they park their campers during elk and deer seasons, a place where a thousand stories have drifted like wisps of smoke around endless campfires. It's a place to which their wives are glad to see them go, glad to be rid of them, glad to be rid of the stories. (For wives, one of the main purposes of hunting camp is to drain off stories.)

I knew that neatly tucked away in the back of Skinny's camper were a couple of tackle boxes, the contents of each compartmentalized, analyzed, and prioritized. He could tell you the fish caught by each lure over the years, not all the fish, of course, way too many of those to keep track of, but the special fish, say anything over two pounds. Make that a pound and a half. Okay, half a pound.

The camper isn't that big but it contains about everything a person might need. Ever.

Useless Person: "We got a tree down across the road up ahead."

Skinny: "I got an ax and a chain saw in the camper. Wait till I fill my pipe and I'll take care of that tree for you."

Useless Person: "I just drove my snowmobile into the creek and can't budge it."

Skinny: "Don't fret, son, I got a block and tackle in the camper."

Useless Person: "My battery's dead."

Skinny: "Now stop banging your head up and down on that engine block, son. I got jumper cables in the camper."

Useless Person: "Man, the only thing that will get us out of this situation is some serious prayer."

Skinny: "No problem. I got two preachers, a priest, and a rabbi in the camper."

Still stalled in the traffic jam, the skinny guy knocked the ash out of his pipe and began running a pipe cleaner in and out of the stem. His gaze drifted in my direction. Our eyes met. He gave a little jump. Embarrassed, he turned his attention back to his pipe, as though cleaning it required serious study, a time bomb on which he had to cut just the right wire. Oh, he knew I was on to him all right. He knew I knew that he had figured it all out.

At lunch that day, I told my attorney, Dicky Scroom, of Scroom & Flee, Attorneys at Law, about the skinny guy in the pickup.

"Guys like that oughta be against the law," Dicky said.

"Yeah," I said. "How do they pull it off?"

"They're smart," he said. "A lot smarter than you or I."

I didn't mind so much hearing that guys like Skinny are smarter than I am, but I didn't like hearing it about my attorney.

"Maybe I should hire one of them," I said.

"Wouldn't take you on. Too smart!"

Driving home later, I kept an eye out for Skinny but didn't see him. I wouldn't have, of course, until the fish had stopped biting. I didn't see any of the other Skinnies either. There's not a lot of them around anymore. I think they're a dying breed. Or maybe the Internet ate 'em, as it has so many of my friends.

"I just bought a car on the Internet," one of them told me gleefully the other day.

"What do you need a car for?" I said. "You think you can drive it on the Information Highway?"

Can you?

I really hate to think the Internet is eating the Skinnies, and I doubt it is. Still, you never know.

Back when I was a kid, half the male population where we lived seemed to be made up of Skinnies. They were men who KNEW THINGS! What kind of things? I don't know, just THINGS. Stop asking questions. Somehow they managed to lead these tidy, self-sufficient, self-reliant lives that allowed them to go off and spend two or three weeks in elk camp down in the Selway every fall, where they stocked up on meat and stories for the winter. They never took me to elk camp with them, they knew better than that, always too smart, but they did take me deer hunting, passing me from hunt to hunt, the Skinnies, although some of them weren't all that skinny by any means.

Hunting and fishing were central to the Skinnies' lives. What everything pretty much came down to was hunting and fishing. The wives of the Skinnies probably thought of themselves as part of the hunting-and-fishing support system.

My own life has never been tidy, not back then, not now. Sometimes when I don't know whether I'm coming or going,

I'll meet myself coming, and it's seldom from fishing. Sometimes I'm beside myself, but we're not going hunting. I suppose that's why my attention fastened like a laser on Skinny in traffic the other day. Here it was the middle of the morning in the middle of the week and this guy was going fishing! He looked so pleased with himself, sitting over there puffing his pipe, calmly contemplating what lure he'd tie on first.

I'd thought maybe I should yell over and tell him about the report I'd read on the health effects of pipe smoking. Got it off the Internet. You know, just a little something for him to meditate on while out in the boat on a truly beautiful day when everyone else is WORKING!

I yelled over at him. "Hey, buddy!"

He glanced back over at me, puzzled, a bit of alarm stirring in his eyebrows.

"Good luck with the fishing!"

What the heck. Somebody's got to do it.

The Gap

A chance passerby on that sunny day in May might easily have assumed that my friends and I had been fired out the door of Delmore Blight Junior High by some kind of powerful, spring-loaded catapult. How else explain the flat, screaming trajectory of those four human projectiles? Surely the observer would have been dumbfounded to learn that the powerful propellant consisted of nothing more than sheer elation over the fact that we had once more, against all expectation, arrived at the last day of school and the beginning of summer vacation.

It has taken me nearly half a century to unravel the mystery of why such a happy event should result in so much misery. The culprit, I've deduced, is the very phrase itself—"summer vacation."

Back then for some reason, summer vacation started much earlier than it does now for my grandchildren, which is only right, because school was much harder in the olden days. Teachers were tougher and meaner. They took no prisoners and no excuses. They hit, too, usually with the flat side of a ruler:

"I just wanted to mention, Mrs. Crankshaft, and you'll get a big kick out of this, I'm sure, that the reason I don't have my homework this morning is . . . !" *whap* ". . . ow! my dog ate it."

After all this time, I think I've finally figured out why the phrase "summer vacation" caused us so much misery. It was The Gap. Summer vacation was like Christmas to the power of ten. Now don't misunderstand me, I loved Christmas vacation. But it possessed the fault of excessive brevity. I was pleased, of course, to get a day off for Washington's birthday. His getting born had proved to be a lasting benefit to the school children of America. The same goes for Lincoln and Columbus and any of those other guys. But individual days honoring the famous and deserving blew by like puffs of wind. They had no staying power. Nobody ever said, "I can hardly wait until George Washington's birthday," because we all knew that *poof!* it would be gone. Summer vacation, on the other hand, stretched out before us like a fat eternity. We couldn't believe we'd ever use it all up. We could spend whole days on absolutely nothing and still feel we'd turned a profit. Summer vacation was simply that big and that glorious.

For whatever reason, the day we got sprung from school for summer vacation usually occurred shortly after mid-May. At least that was the case the day my friends and I were propelled out of seventh grade and the front door of Delmore Blight Junior High. We alit on the outskirts of town, skidded to a stop, and flopped down on the warm, steamy earth to take stock of our good fortune, the riches of time that had suddenly been thrust upon us.

"Hey, you know what?" said Birdy Thompson. "We should celebrate by taking a swim in Sand Crick."

"Great idea!" shouted Retch Sweeney.

"Super!" cried Sid Benson.

"Wait a minute," I said. "Don't you think it's a little early for swimming?"

"Geez," Retch said. "Are you some kind of twerp or what? Tell me, what day is today, Patrick?"

"The start of summer vacation."

"Right. *Summer* vacation. And what do we do in the summer, guys?"

"We swim!" shouted Sid and Birdy.

"Yea!" I said.

And there, you see, was The Gap. Between the start of summer vacation and the start of actual summer gapped a whole month. It was the word "summer" in summer vacation that proved so inviting, so deceptive, particularly to my friends with IQs approximating that of concrete. I don't mean to insult them. Dumb guys, I've found, generally make the best friends, because they're so much more interesting and exciting than smart guys, those guys who have the intelligence to recognize such a phenomenon as The Gap for what it is and stay home to tidy up their stamp and coin collections.

"Yea," I repeated. "Oh wait. I just thought of something. We can't go swimming. We don't have our swimming suits."

At that the guys all hooted and hollered and scrambled to their feet so they could actually fall down laughing.

"Swimming suits!" squeaked Birdy in the throes of mirth. "We don't need swimming suits! We'll skinny-dip!"

"Skinny-dip," I said. "I had forgotten about that. Yea."

It is here that I must admit something truly embarrassing. I suppose it is a psychosis of some kind, the result of being raised in an extremely prudish family. As far as I know, nobody in my family got naked. Ever. Perhaps that is why I was a good deal less than happy with the prospect of getting naked with my friends—these friends in particular. Believe me, psychosis is not all bad.

In far less time than I had hoped for, we arrived at a high, grassy bank rising steeply above Sand Creek. The water appeared clear and inviting. This was because the spring runoff hadn't started yet. Up until today the weather had been too cold.

As I stared down into the rippling current I made some rapid calculations. The creek flowed out of a mountain canyon approximately a mile from my house. The canyon stretched approximately two miles up to the peaks still clogged with ice and snow. Three miles in all. I estimated the flow of the current to be about three miles an hour. That meant that perhaps slightly more than an hour ago this water had been transformed from ice and snow.

"Last one in is a rotten egg!" yelled Retch.

He, Birdy, and Sid raced to kick off their shoes and strip off their clothes until, still wearing their winter pallor, they soon resembled three peeled bananas cavorting about.

I should mention here that I also did not particularly care for the sight of naked guys cavorting about. Girls were another matter. True, I had never seen one of them naked, much less cavorting in that condition, but I'd heard favorable rumors.

"I said, 'Last one in is a rotten egg!'" Retch repeated for my benefit.

Being a rotten egg registered on my fear scale somewhere between being late for piano practice and last in line on liver soup day. "Hey, wait for me, guys," I yelled back. "I can't get my shoes untied."

"Har har," they laughed. "He can't get his shoes untied!"

"No fair, guys," I yelled.

"Too late!" Retch shouted. "I'm going in!" He leaped from the bank. "GerrrronnnnaMOEEEEIIIIIIIII!"

Sid and Birdy appeared a good deal troubled by Retch's report concerning the temperature of the water. They both decided, quite sensibly, not to follow him in. Unfortunately, they had already launched themselves from the high bank. They turned in midair and tried to return to the bank by means of a frenzied flailing of arms and legs. It appeared to me that they briefly gained a few inches of altitude but then, possibly because of a downdraft, they soon lost it. Their screams were truly heartrending, particularly considering that they hadn't hit the water yet.

I walked to edge of the bank and looked down, any embarrassment over my being the rotten egg quickly dissipating. The three fresh eggs, so to speak, were desperately clawing at the sandy bank, apparently hoping to extract themselves from the frigid creek by tunneling upward to freedom.

"There's a beach a few hundred yards downstream," I told them. "You can get out there."

I waved as they gave up tunneling and drifted away. They did not wave back. As their shrieks faded to silence, it occurred to me that the beach was on the far side of the creek. To get back to their clothes, they would either have to float another several hundred yards more to the next beach or hike down to the county road bridge and cross there.

Daffy old Mrs. Swisher happened to be driving across the bridge a short while later. As soon as she got home, she called my mom. I happened at that moment to be sipping a cup of hot cocoa and tidying up my stamp collection.

"You mean they were naked?" Mom gasped. "Retch Sweeney, Birdy Thompson, and Sid Benson?" She listened a moment. "Oh, they weren't naked. . . . They were wearing pale blue leotards. . . . I see. . . . No, no, I don't think it would be a good idea to tell Mr. Sweeney. He'll find out soon enough."

A couple of days later we were sprawled in the Sweeney backyard. "We need to think of something to do," Birdy complained. "We can't just lie here all summer."

"I got an idea," Retch said. "Let's go camping!"

"Great idea!" shouted Sid.

"Camping?" I said.

"Sure," said Birdy. "Hey, it's summer vacation. What do we do in summer? We go camping!"

"Yea," I said.

A few nights later I was lying on the ground in my

chicken-down sleeping bag a couple of miles up Sand Creek Canyon.

"What are you doing?" Retch asked me.

"Watching mosquitoes freeze to death on my skin," I said.

"Me too," Retch said. "You notice how they make funny little tinkling sounds when you flick them off?"

"I can't feel my legs!" Birdy cried out. "I can't feel my legs!"

"I wonder how come it's so cold," Sid wondered aloud. "It being summer vacation and all."

I had no answer. It would be forty years before I figured out The Gap.

Incident at Fish Camp

Nobody wanted the Old Man in Fish Camp. He was obnoxious, self-centered, opinionated, arrogant, inconsiderate, irascible, demanding, and careless with the truth. But those were not the reasons we didn't want him in Fish Camp. We other participants in Fish Camp shared many of those same characteristics, and were therefore tolerant of them. The problem was, the Old Man cheated at cards. All the rest of us cheated at cards, too, but the Old Man was good at it. He didn't cheat fair.

Still, we couldn't slip away without him, not because we'd feel guilty but because we couldn't afford to leave him alone with our wives. They think the old geezer is cute and charming, the last of the truly suave and chivalrous gentlemen, and they spoil him. In exchange, he tells them outrageous lies about us. That is why we can't afford to leave him home, which is too bad, because otherwise the terrifying and disgusting incident at Fish Camp might never have happened.

When I refer to the Old Man as "old," I mean *really old*. He's probably a hundred or more, but nobody knows for sure because he lies about everything, including his age. He's now but a wisp of his former self, the former self being pretty wispy in the first place. He also nurtures an extremely high opinion of himself.

"I think you boys should venerate me," he said as we were driving up to Fish Camp.

"Ventilate you?" Retch Sweeney said. "You're already too ventilated."

"Venerate!" the Old Man shouted. "It means, you ignorami, that you should honor me. It ain't easy being this old!"

"It ain't easy having you be that old!"

They went on like that for an hour and more and were about to drive us over the edge, until Pete Kelly shouted out, "You're about to drive us over the edge!" Startled out of a retort, Retch managed to whip the car back onto the road.

"The two of you knock it off," I told Retch and the Old Man. "We're going up to Fish Camp to relax and enjoy ourselves."

That's when young Barney Felton spoke up. "And fish!"

This was his first trip to Fish Camp with us, so Barney wasn't familiar with the regular routine.

"Fish?" Al Finley said. "What do you mean, 'fish'? We don't go up to Fish Camp to *fish*."

"We don't?" Barney said. "Why else would we go to a place called 'Fish Camp'?"

At that all the regulars burst out laughing. Youngsters nowadays get some of the strangest ideas. The Internet must be sucking atoms out of their brains.

"Barney," I explained kindly, "if we wanted to fish, we certainly wouldn't go to Fish Camp. We'd go someplace where there are fish. Why in the world would you expect fish near a place called 'Fish Camp'? It doesn't make sense."

"It doesn't? I guess maybe it was just a crazy idea that popped into my head. What is it we do at Fish Camp then?"

The Old Man adjusted his spectacles and peered over the top of them at Barney, as though studying a newly discovered but fairly unpleasant life-form. "Well, son, I'll tell you what we do. We take turns reading the classics to each other, discuss philosophy and art, and recite poetry. By then we're so worked up with the excitement of it all, there's no way we can get to sleep. That's when we put on some opera to calm us all down."

"Stop the car!" Barney shouted. "I want out!"

"Whoa there, Barney," I said. "Old Ed is making Fish Camp sound a whole lot wilder than it actually is. I'll admit that on occasion a fight breaks out between the Freudians and the Jungians, but that's a rarity. You don't have to worry too much about that kind of rough stuff."

"I hope not," Barney said. "Anyway, I don't think you should call the place Fish Camp if you don't fish there."

"We don't always call it Fish Camp," I said. "In September we call it Grouse Camp or maybe Elk Camp. October, it's Deer Camp. Fish Camp is basically a state of mind."

I should mention here that the Fish Camp cabin is a duplex of sorts, each side having its own door, bathroom, and wood stove. We do our cultural and social activities on one side and our sleeping, what there is of it, on the other, which is pretty much jammed full of bunks.

One of our rules is that everyone helps keep the place tidy, but we did have a scare not too long ago. Wally Finch, the game warden, said he had stopped by Fish Camp and it looked as if some bears or other large animals had broken in and hibernated there for the winter. We were shocked. A couple of the boys were immediately dispatched to check out the situation, and they reported back that the game warden must have been hallucinating—Fish Camp was just the way we left it. Needless to say, we worried for quite a while about Wally's state of mind, but he seems all right now.

Anyway, I started out to tell about the incident at Fish

Camp. The sequence of events gets pretty complicated, but I will attempt to reconstruct it as best I can, starting with our first night.

As usual, the Old Man cheated us out of all of our money at poker, which we had, uh, managed to sandwich in between the poetry readings and the opera. Then Old Ed claimed to be all tuckered out and went off to bed. Now that he'd got all our money, he had to figure out some way to spend it before we could win it back, not that there's much chance of that. Once alone in the bunk room he got on his cell phone and called one of his girlfriends, Lulu Swartz. Then he sneaked off down the road a couple hundred yards, so his rendezvous with Lulu couldn't be detected. Lulu flew out in her big old silver town car and picked him up. Lulu, at a mere eighty-two, is practically a spring chicken.

We didn't realize the rapscallion was gone until the next morning. By lunch he still hadn't shown up.

"He probably went looking for mushrooms and got lost," Barney said. "I'm worried."

"Yeah, I'm worried sick, too," Retch said. "Pass the potatoes."

"We better go find him," Barney said. "The temperature's gonna drop below freezing tonight."

"Any more bacon?" Pete Kelly asked, his forehead furrowed with concern.

"I'll tell you this, Barney," I said. "The Old Man isn't lost. He may be dead but he ain't lost."

"Dead!" exclaimed Barney. "You really think so?"

"I don't discount it. He's at least a hundred."

"You wanna know what I think?" Pete Kelly said.

"What?" said Barney, leaning forward, eager for any encouragement at all.

"I think," said Pete, "that this coffee is eating the lining out of my stomach. Good, though."

Three nights came and went with no sign of the Old Man.

At one point we had a hundred searchers in the woods, three TV news crews at the cabin, and one National Guard helicopter rotating overhead.

"I think Old Ed's a goner," the sheriff said on the third evening. "I'm calling off the search."

"Well, I'm not leavin' him out there as a feast for the coyotes," Barney blurted out. "I'm gonna keep looking till I find him."

It took Lulu three days to get sick and tired of the Old Man. She drove him back to Fish Camp, booted him out, and roared off home. Ed got up, dusted himself off, and sauntered into the cabin to tell us about his adventures.

"Nothing at all improper happened," he explained. "Otherwise, I had a pretty good time."

He was pleased as punch when we told him about the search for his worthless old carcass. When Ed heard Barney was still out looking for him, he laughed himself into near exhaustion and went off to bed in the bunk section still chuckling.

Sometime after dark, Barney returned to camp. He stumbled into the bunk room, and the first thing he saw was Old Ed stretched out on a bunk. Realizing there was no way Ed could have survived three freezing nights in the woods, Barney assumed we had found Old Ed's body and returned it to camp. He grabbed his flashlight and shined it into Ed's face. As he did so, a great sadness came upon him, because up to that point he still retained a fondness for the Old Man.

What Barney didn't realize was that the beam of the flashlight penetrated Old Ed's paper-thin eyelids. Ed slowly became aware of a bright light seemingly coming closer and closer, getting brighter and brighter. *Good gosh!* he thought. *I've died and gone to heaven!* He panicked. Emitting a frightened squawk, he bolted upright in the bunk and right into Barney's face.

That's when we heard what can only be described as a series of high-pitched barks, the kind of eerie sounds that starve the heart of blood and stir the hairs on the back of the neck. Boots thundered across the floor, followed by a crash, then a wavering, high-pitched screech. We ran outside, unsure whether to investigate or try to escape, every man for himself. But then we saw it: an image so horrible and disgusting grown men retched and turned away in an effort to avoid brain damage. For standing there in the gaping doorway of the bunk room, bathed in pearly white moonlight, stood the Old Man, skinny as a rail and stark naked, shaking his fist at the diminishing sounds of a person in full flight through the woods.

"For gosh sakes, Ed!" I yelled. "What happened?"

"I died," he said. "I died and went to heaven, but they kicked me back out."

"Small wonder," I said. "What happened to the door?"

"I don't know. By the time I got back in my body and opened my eyes, this big hairy creature was bending over me, an inch from my face."

"What kind of creature?"

"I don't know but it had big bulging eyes, big white teeth set in a jaw that sagged halfway to the floor, and a screech that was almost human. Smelled real bad, too. It must have torn off the door on its way out. Oh it was an ugly thing, I'll tell you that."

Retch shrugged. "Barney. It's gotta be Barney."

"Gotta be," I said. "Well, he'll be back. I just hope he remembers to bring the door."

"My nerves are shot," said the Old Man. "You two stop your yappin' and go put on the opera."

Roughing It Over Easy

Our rich friend Fenton Quagmire picked up Retch Sweeney and me for a little outing up in the Cabinet Mountains. We were disappointed to learn that we had to rough it.

"How come you didn't bring the nice motor home instead of this old clunker, Quagmire?" Retch asked. "Think the new one was too good for your low-class friends?"

"Low-class?" Quagmire said. "Who promoted you guys?"

"Hey, Quagmire," I said. "It's not that we have anything against your two-hundred-thousand dollar rig here. It's perfectly fine for roughing it in the mountains. We certainly can get by on the bare necessities—the standard-size TV, the microwave, the air-conditioning, and the like. It's just, you know, we get used to the first-class treatment when we go camping with you."

"You're right," Quagmire said. "Actually, I'm a little embarrassed to be seen in the Old Grunge here. It's already three years old. But I had to put the new rig in the shop. The humidity control seemed to be acting up. Just lucky I held on to this old thing."

"You did right," I said. "Think what might have happened if we'd been way off somewhere in the mountains and the humidity control conked out."

"Gives me the shakes just thinking about it," Retch said.

I picked up a caviar hors d'oeuvre off the tray on the coffee table. Retch slipped the video of *The Magnificent Seven* into the cassette player and stretched out on the couch. I thought about popping a bag of popcorn into the microwave but decided to wait. You never know what kind of delicacies Quagmire might have in the freezer, so it's not a good idea to take the edge off your appetite too soon. I spun the captain's chair around a couple of times, making myself either slightly dizzy or reflective.

"Either of you guys remember back when we'd go on an outing and actually go out?"

"What?" Retch said. "You mean go outside?"

"Like out in the elements?" Quagmire added.

"I bet you guys don't even remember campfires." I said. "In the evening we'd sit around the campfire and poke at it with sticks."

"Why would we do that?" Quagmire asked. "Poke at the fire with sticks?"

"I don't know," I said. "We just did it. That's what you did in the evening with a campfire."

"Didn't the smoke get in the way of us watching TV?" Retch asked.

"No," I said. "Because there wasn't any TV. There would just be us and our sleeping bags and maybe a tent."

"And mosquitoes and deer flies," Retch said, popping a grape into his mouth. "I do seem to remember mosquitoes and deer flies."

"Wind and rain," Quagmire said. "I remember that storm on the side of a mountain one night when we thought the tent was going to turn into a hang glider! Boy, that was fun."

We were starting to wind up a narrow mountain road with numerous switchbacks and large rocks scattered about. I was glad Quagmire was driving. And that it was his rig. This was about the last place in the world I'd want to meet a loaded logging truck and have to back up a motor home around all these hairpin curves.

"Say what you want about actually going out when you go out, but I like this," Retch said, rubbing the soft nap on the upholstery as if it were his banky. Suddenly, he pointed out a window. "Hey, what's the name of that peak over there?"

"Mount Horrible," I said.

"I thought Mount Horrible was down in the Blues. Ain't that where we nearly froze to death back in the olden days?"

"Which time we nearly froze to death? Be more specific."

"Well, let's see. Oh, yeah, it was the time we ran out of water and had to drink out of mud puddles in that old skid trail. I can still remember sifting out the pebbles with my teeth."

"That was Mount Misery."

"You're right. That's when we hiked out through Starvation Flats."

"And you broke through the ice crossing Deadman's Creek! Funny!"

"Hey, will you guys please stop it?" Quagmire pleaded. "Mount Horrible, Mount Misery, Starvation Flats, Deadman's Creek! You're starting to depress me. Where do these dreadful names come from, anyway?"

" 'They're certainly P. M. H.," I said.

"P. M. H.?"

"Pre motor home."

"It's them old-time campers what done it," Retch said. "Come up with these names. Life was tough back then. There was no pussyfootin' around when it came to naming stuff."

"You ever get the feeling," said Quagmire, "that old-time campers weren't a bundle of laughs."

"Yeah," I said, swiveling around in my captain's chair to nip another canape off the coffee table. "But it's not as if we don't have our own hardships. Just suppose you had brought your *nice* rig, Quagmire, and the humidity control had gone out on us."

"Makes me shudder," said Retch. "But I guess that's why we come on these adventures, just to expose ourselves to such risks."

"Sure," I said. "We really do expose ourselves to risks and hardships out here in the wilds. I think we should start renaming the local geographic features to reflect our own hardships."

"Dang right," Retch said.

"I'm all for it," said Quagmire. "You go first, Pat. Give us a new name for Mount Misery."

"All right, let's see now. Hmmm. Okay, how about In-Denial Peak?"

"Perfect!" exclaimed Quagmire. "Your turn, Retch. A new name for Mount Horrible."

"This is hard. Um, how about, uh, Mount Alimony?"

"Not bad," I said. "Your turn, Quagmire."

"One-Trip-Only Buffet Flats!"

"Attention-Deficit-Disorder Hill."

"Co-Dependency Gulch!"

"Irregularity Creek!"

"Pattern-Baldness Mountain!"

"Stop!" I cried at last. "I can't stand it! I'm sorry I ever came up with the idea!"

"Summer-Rerun Springs!" yelled Quagmire.

"High-Cholesterol Pass!" cried Retch.

"Stop it!" I shouted again. "Let's face it. We're not in the same league as old-time campers, when it comes to danger and hardship."

"Logging Truck . . . !" Retch shouted.

"Didn't you hear me tell you to stop . . . LOGGING TRUCK!"

Quagmire swallowed a caviar canape whole, stood on the brakes, threw the motor home into reverse, and sent it roaring and screeching backward down and around three switchbacks before he skidded it into a turnout. The long silence that followed was marred only by heavy breathing and a light dripping of cold sweat. Retch at last spoke.

"New name for road: Change-Your-Shorts—!"

"Forget it," I said. "We're just going to let the old names stand. They tell you something about life back in the olden days. You take Mount Misery. A hunting party was stranded up there in a blizzard and—"

"Forget Mount Misery," Quagmire said. "Here's some real misery for you guys. We must have knocked out the oil pan on the motor home. You two have to walk back to town and get a wrecker."

"Don't try to kid us, Quagmire," I said. "Just call on your cell phone."

"Tried it. Doesn't work down in this canyon. Ditto the CB. So you guys are walking!"

"Try and make us, Quagmire!"

Fortunately, the moon came up shortly after dark, and Retch and I had no trouble finding our way down the road.

"I don't mind roughing it," Retch said. "But this is ridiculous. Walking! Outdoors! At night! You wouldn't think Quagmire would be so mean as to threaten not to let us camp in his new motor home anymore, would you?"

"No," I said. "But that's the problem with some of these rich guys. They can be ruthless when they want to."

"We should teach him a good lesson. He can just keep his old motor home. We'll dig the old IFUT out of my garage and go camping with it?"

"I forget," I said. "What's an IFUT?"

"The old interior-frame umbrella tent. You know, where you held up the frame by resting the end of the little pipe on the top of your head, and it cut little donut holes out of your scalp while you were putting together the rest of the tent frame. And we could sleep right on the hard, cold ground, just like in the old days, and burn our food over a campfire. It would be fun, wouldn't it, to go on an outing where we actually go out? Ha! Just kidding!"

"That's a relief," I said. "For a minute there, I thought the hardship of walking down this road had driven you stark-raving mad."

Culinary Magic

If I do say so myself, I'm a pretty fair camp cook, although I do have my detractors, one of whom happens to be my very own grandson Daniel. Just recently, feigning an expression of incredulity, Daniel stared at the plat du jour I had just set before him. Anticipating his response, I offered a few words of encouragement: "Shut up and eat."

"Aaii! What is it?" he asked, thrusting the plate away.

"Spaghetti," I told him.

"What's on top of it?"

"Chili."

"This is a joke, right? A *mean* joke."

"No," I said. "It's my latest culinary invention. You like spaghetti, don't you?"

"Yeah, but—"

"And you like chili, don't you?"

"Yeah, but—"

"Well, there you go. It's only logical that you must

therefore like spaghetti topped with chili. So stop whining and eat your breakfast."

Of course when he got home, Daniel immediately blabbed to his mother, my daughter, that he had been forced to eat spaghetti topped with chili.

"Stop complaining," she said. "It has to be better than Dad's wiener stew."

Geez, wiener stew. I haven't had any of that in ages. May have to whip up a batch.

I got my start as a camp cook at about age eight. I had bought a little fold-up stove from Grogan's War Surplus. Folded up, the stove was about the size of a deck of cards. Unfolded, it was also about the size of a deck of cards. The fuel for the stove consisted of some white tablets that smelled like lighter fluid.

On the day of my first venture into camp cookery, Crazy Eddie Muldoon and I had caught three or four little trout and decided to cook them alongside the stream. Usually, Eddie reserved any fun new project for himself, but a week or two earlier he had accidentally managed to ignite a pile of stumps into a raging inferno. The fire itself had died out after a few days, but, as Eddie reported, his rear end still radiated an afterglow. He said his nerves weren't up to dealing with matches anytime soon. I assumed the nerves he referred to were those associated with his posterior.

"No problem," I said, whipping the little stove out of my pocket. "I'll cook our fish myself."

And I did. I lit the fuel tablet and held the little fish over it on a sharpened stick until they turned a nice golden brown. The experiment was slightly marred when one of the fish fell off the stick and landed on the flaming fuel tablet. I deftly flipped it off the tablet into the sand, wiped it on my pants, and gave it to Eddie. He ate it. He said it tasted pretty good, but could have used a little less sand and a little more salt. A short while later, he reported a strange sensation. He said it was hard to describe but sort of felt as if an ice pick had been stuck through his head. Other than that, he experienced no ill effects, except years later he had recurring dreams about becoming a life insurance agent. It makes you wonder.

I ate the rest of the fish. They tasted pretty darn good, too, particularly if you like the flavor of lighter fluid as much as I do. As you can see, I experienced no lasting ill effects. As you can see, I experienced no lasting ill effects. As you can see, I experienced . . . Wait. Where was I?

By age twelve, my camping had become much more elaborate. I had purchased one of everything from Grogan's War Surplus, and I carried every last speck of it on every camping trip. I looked like an army supply depot creeping up the trail toward camp. Other hikers didn't even realize there was a small human somewhere inside the pile. ("Good Lord, Martha, run! It's starting to move!") But let me tell you, once I got to camp I was prepared. If one of the guys had trouble starting the campfire, I'd say, "Stand aside." Then I'd give his pitiful pile of smoldering sticks a shot from my flamethrower. No, only kidding about that. I didn't have a flamethrower. That and a Sherman tank were about the only things Grogan wouldn't sell me. I dreamed of driving my tank across the countryside, every so often blasting something with the flamethrower. Some of our old neighbors back then claimed they dreamed the same thing about me. Talk about your coincidences.

After my friends and I finally arrived at our campsite, we'd get all our stuff neatly arranged in windrows, and then we'd start to cook. All of our grub, by the way, was carried in its natural state—milk, eggs, juice, fruit, whatever. Dehydrated stuff was for sissies. Real campers carried their food with the water still in it.

Kids, here's a backpacking tip for you: I carried the fresh eggs wrapped up in my extra pair of underwear to keep them from breaking. This proved to be highly efficient, because the eggs always broke anyway. So if I wanted to make scrambled eggs, I'd just wring my underwear out over the frying pan, leaving the shells screened out by the underwear! It was neat.

"Who wants scrambled eggs?" I'd ask.

"Not me."

"Count me out."

"Not a chance."

Actually, I made scrambled eggs only the one time, because none of the other guys seemed to like them. My mother's reaction when I got home didn't help either. The thought of that piercing screech still sends shivers up my spine.

My first attempt at baking pancakes on a camping trip turned out spectacularly. My friends talk about those pancakes even to this day. Retch Sweeney claims he still has a couple of them around. He says his wife uses them for hot pads. I think he's joking, but it hurts my feelings anyway.

Speaking of hurt feelings, I'm reminded of my first effort to bake bread in a reflector oven. I made the oven out of foil and a framework of sticks. The dough was the tricky part. I had a terrible time achieving the right consistency. First I'd get too much flour, then too much water, then too much flour. By the time I was finished, the dough had engulfed half our campsite, devouring sleeping bags, tents, napping campers. Ignoring the muffled screams ("No! No! Stay away from me! Aiiii!"), I patted out the dough into roughly the shape of a loaf of bread, which I then plopped into the reflector oven. (Another camping tip: Kids, if you want to get your hands really clean, pat out a big ball of bread dough.)

That loaf of bread turned out hard as a rock and about twice as heavy, but remained perfectly white. It was impervious to heat. If I hadn't been so disappointed, and humiliated, I might have saved the recipe and patented it as a formula for a heat-resistant substance. For example, NASA could have prevented a spacecraft from burning up on reentry to Earth's atmosphere by coating it with my bread dough.

"NASA to space shuttle. How's the bread-dough shield holding up?"

"Fine! It has deflected several large flaming meteors but remains unmarred and is still perfectly white."

What really hurt, though, was that my so-called friends grabbed up my loaf of bread and began throwing it back and forth like a football, until Norm pointed out someone might get hit in the head with it and killed. I could almost see the headline: BOY STRUCK DOWN BY LOAF OF BREAD.

Later I made some biscuits with the same dough. Which reminds me. Half a century later some Cub Scouts investigated that very same camping spot.

"Hey, look at this rock," one of them said. "It's shaped exactly like a biscuit. A pure white biscuit!"

"Here's another one!" someone else yelled. "It's shaped exactly like a biscuit, too."

"I found one!"

"Me, too!"

"Maybe they're not rocks," the first Cub yelled. "Maybe they're dinosaur eggs! Maybe they're about ready to hatch out a bunch of vicious little raptors! Let's get out of here!"

Well, it's a darn good thing they did get out of there. Suppose those Cubs got to fooling around and started throwing the dinosaur eggs at each other. Someone might have got hit in the head and seriously injured. Dinosaur eggs are really hard. But as I started to say about my biscuits, I thought they turned out pretty well, considering it was my first attempt at baking them. Of course, you can't expect any first attempt to be perfect.

People keep telling me I should write a cookbook. Come to think of it, maybe only one person told me that. Can't remember who it was right now. Oh, yeah, it was my grandson Daniel. After he'd finished his breakfast of spaghetti-topped-with-chili, I said, "There now, that wasn't so bad, was it?"

"Yum," he said. "Maybe you should write a cookbook."

No kidding, those were his exact words.

If I May Digress

When I drove down to our little local post office the other day to pick up the mail, I noticed a number of pickups parked around the building, which isn't all that odd here in Blight, Idaho, because most folks here drive a pickup truck, usually with a chain saw in the bed, just in case a tree falls across the road behind you while you've gone to get the mail, scarcely what I'd call a rare occurrence what with all the beavers we got in the river now, and let me tell you there's nothing a beaver likes better than to drop a cottonwood across the road behind you and cut you off from home any chance it gets, cottonwoods naturally being the favorite tree of beavers for this purpose, although if a cottonwood isn't handy a beaver will take just about any tree, even a bull pine with a bad taste, if he has his heart set on dropping a tree across the road, but the beavers usually have two or three cottonwoods gnawed down to a spike not much bigger than a toothpick, a beaver version of a hair trigger, and all they have

to do is give the spike a chomp or two and a big old cottonwood flops down behind you when you've gone to get the
mail, so you see there was nothing unusual about a bunch of
pickup trucks parked in front of the post office, except there
wasn't a soul in sight, and that did seem strange, because
almost always some of the boys are standing around chewing
the fat, the mail run being about the only opportunity most of
us have for a little socializing and to catch up on the gossip,
not that we have a lot of gossip but occasionally someone
comes up with a juicy bit that makes the mail run worth the
trouble, so I'm starting to wonder if maybe I've stumbled into
Rod Serling's *Twilight Zone*, which you no doubt remember
because that was about the best TV program ever, a real
spooky show and certainly a far cry from all these sitcoms
they got on the tube nowadays where a bunch of boys and
girls scarcely out of their teens cavort together in an apartment in New York City, hardly any of them seeming to do a
lick of real work, and all they ever talk or think about is sex,
something my own mother never let me talk or think about
until I was about forty-seven years old, ha ha, and had a real
job, well sort of a real job, the pay not being all that much,
except in those days you could go to a movie and buy a box of
popcorn and a soda without doing serious injury to a dollar
bill, but as I was saying, I'm starting to get a little nervous,
there not being a single person anywhere in sight right during the rush hour at the post office, and I sat there in my
pickup truck for five minutes or more, trying to size up the
situation, because that's the way I am, careful to weigh the
risk before making my move, always have been that way,
even when I was a pup, because I'd learned early on that caution pays, particularly when it's dark outside, not that I was
ever afraid of the dark, mind you, just careful, ha ha, but I'll
tell you this, it has certainly paid off when it comes to hunting and fishing, where you can mess up big time if you're constantly rushing hither and thither and never take the time to
size up a situation, like just last week when I suspected there

might be a big rainbow trout tucked away under a sub-
merged log and if I had just rushed in willy-nilly I would have
spooked it for sure before I even got a fly in the water, if there
had actually been a big rainbow under the log, but you get
my drift, caution pays off, and that is why I was taking my
time to check out the peculiar situation at the post office, and
you know, why, it was just as if the drivers of those pickup
trucks had been snatched up by an alien spaceship, which I
don't actually believe in very much, but like I say, caution
does pay off, because just as I was about to get out of my
truck I noticed something peculiar, none other than Charlie
Fipps hiding behind a bush in front of the post office, and I
says to myself, "What on earth is he up to?" and I scrunched
way down in my seat and glanced around and that's when I
noticed Bert Hawkins flattened back into a little impression
on the side wall of the post office, and then I detected the
crown of Farley Sheppard's cowboy hat poking up on the
driver's side of his pickup, and it was pretty clear Farley was
under the hat, all mighty mysterious, I can tell you that, but
scarcely a second later I flashed on the solution to the mystery, and it was that everyone was in hiding because parked
right next to me was old Skeeter Gibson's pickup, oh, but
don't get me wrong, old Skeeter is as nice a guy as you're
likely to come across, give you the shirt off his back, but if he
catches sight of you he will talk your ear off for hours on end
without so much as a pause to catch his breath or allow you
to get a word in edgewise to let him know you have to go to
the bathroom or to a funeral or whatever, because old
Skeeter scarcely gets to the end of one sentence before he is
deep into another, a technique of digression he has mastered
to the point where one episode merges seamlessly with
another, leaving the listener no opportunity to escape even
between stories, and so I scrunched down even more until I
could just barely peep over the dashboard, and sure enough,
a few moments later Skeeter emerges from the post office,
glances about for a potential listener, finds none, not even

me, because I'd tucked myself so far down under the dash I had the brake pedal gouging me in the ribs, and then Skeeter got in his truck and drove off, which struck me as kind of sad, actually.

But still everyone remained in hiding, mighty peculiar if you ask me, and I figured something was afoot here, and I said to myself, I don't want to buy into this, and I started my pickup and headed for home, because one can't be too careful, particularly when confronting such odd circumstances, although when I was no more than a block away from the post office I glanced in my rearview mirror and noticed that everybody was coming out from their hiding places, so I guess the emergency or whatever it was had resolved itself, and for a moment I thought about going back and chewing the fat with the boys, telling them a few stories, the boys they get a big kick out of my stories, but I knew by now the beavers would be hard at work on the cottonwoods alongside the river road and you can't be too careful when it comes to beavers.

Just Like Old Times

The spring runoff had just started and the river was tricky. It's always tricky but it was trickier now.

One Norman E. Nelson was steering my boat expertly up the river, playing the fifteen-horse outboard trolling motor like a violin. I wished he would just steer, but that's Norm for you. Everything he does, he does with style.

There was a time when Norm knew the river better than just about anyone, could even predict the strikes: "We'll pick up a good dolly in that hole off the gravel bar." And we would! It was amazing. Magic. Today, though, the old magic wasn't working. The holes weren't where they used to be. Neither were the fish. Rivers change. People change.

Norm had changed. He was still the maestro of the outboard, conducting us upriver, but it was as if no vestige remained of the Norm I once knew a half century ago. What happened? Was this calm, distinguished, even courtly gentleman the same Norm I knew as a kid growing up poor in Idaho? No, it couldn't be. This dapper fellow steering the boat, an elder in his Jehovah's Witnesses church, a renowned public speaker, a history buff who could actually remember dates, surely he must be a Norm Nelson impostor. My mind flashed back, seeking clues to identity.

SCENE: I'm standing on the back porch of Norm's house. I'm about twelve, Norm two years younger. He's what in those days we called "a little fat kid."

A minute or two earlier he had done something to annoy me; I forget what. He's been trying to keep a safe distance from me, but now he's overcome by curiosity.

"What did you just do?" he asks.

"Fixed this thing here."

"What thing?"

"This apple."

"What did you do to it?"

"Inserted a firecracker."

"Why did . . . Oh!"

Even now, in my mind's eye, I see the little fat kid racing for cover, trying to put the Nelsons' apple tree between him and me. But he started too late. The lobbed apple grenade lands inches behind him—I had miscalculated the lead. But just then his feet shoot out from under him and he sits down smack on the apple grenade! Perfect! He flails about, seeking traction on the slick grass, but he can't get off the grenade!

His mother sticks her head out the back door. "For heaven's sake, Normy, stop that screeching!"

I explain: "He's just playacting, Mrs. Nelson."

She shakes her head and goes back to the kitchen.

WHUMMPP!

Normy rises a good two inches into the air. Later, his mother grounds him for ruining his good pants.

SCENE: Norm and I have been out hunting grouse all day. He claims to be dying of thirst. He won't shut up about how thirsty he is. He keeps it up until I'm dying of thirst, too.

"Boy, what I wouldn't give for a great big bottle of pop right now!" Norm says.

We come out of the woods onto a little country road. Right next to the road is a quart-size, unopened, glass bottle of ginger ale sitting in the weeds. Norm grabs it up, pops the cap off with his thumb, and begins to chugalug it.

"Whew," he says, pausing to belch comically and to wipe his chin. "Talk about your miracles! Imagine, a full bottle of ginger ale way out here in the middle of nowhere! Ask and you shall receive! Want a swig?"

"Naw," I say. "To tell you the truth, Norm, I don't think that bottle of ginger ale is the Lord's doing. You popped the lid off that bottle awful easy. Now call to mind, if you will, those ornery Scragg boys who live just up the road. Suppose they saw us go into the woods and . . . !"

I must say it wasn't more than a week before Norm's complexion faded from dark green into a rather nice pastel shade. His choking and gagging subsided soon after.

SCENE: Kenny Thompson, Vern Schulze, Norm, and I have hiked high up into the Selkirk Mountains looking for a lake we'd heard about. Before we get to the lake, a blizzard blows in and catches us on the side of a mountain so steep we can barely stand up.

Norm offers this bit of survival advice: "We better make camp here. We can tie ourselves to trees so we won't fall off the mountain."

We never take the little fat kid's advice on anything. Instead, we retreat to a tiny cabin a trapper had built back in the last century. The blizzard keeps us holed up there for four days. (Every night of which I dream that I'm tied to a tree on the side of the mountain in a blizzard. Norm is responsible for some of my worst dreams.)

One of the features of the trapper's cabin is a little sheet-metal stove with a stovepipe that stops short of the roof by about a foot and a half. The fact that the stovepipe doesn't go through the hole in the roof or even all the way up to it is not regarded by us as a matter of any consequence. Having the roof frequently catch fire as we sit out the blizzard is about our only entertainment.

On the second day of the storm, Kenny and I decide, blizzard or no blizzard, that we are going to venture out and find the lake. We return three hours later half frozen. We strip off all of our icy clothes and sit down naked side by side on the six-inch-high woodpile next to the stove. The heat radiating off of the white-hot stovepipe feels wonderful as we begin to relate our adventure. I can't remember now whether Kenny and I ever found the lake, which normally would be something that might stand out in a person's mind. Perhaps it's what happened next that erased that event from my memory.

Engrossed in telling the tale, I notice out of the corner of my eye that Kenny is violently shaking his head and appears to be trying to speak, but nothing is coming out. Then I look at Norm. He is poised to shoot a free throw with a hard-boiled egg. The "basket" is the opening in the top of the stovepipe! "NOOOOOOOO!" Kenny and I scream in unison. But it's too late. The egg is already arcing toward the stovepipe. With a faint *plip* it lands right on the sharp edge of the pipe. It sticks on the rim.

Before I can move, the sizzling, white-hot stovepipe topples toward my naked lap. Not being stupid, I catch the pipe in my hands. Kenny is straining to rise from the pile of firewood. I hand him the pipe. He sits back down and hands the pipe to me. I hand it back to him. In the brief intervals one of us isn't holding the pipe, we try to escape from the woodpile, but it's too low. I have no idea how many times that stovepipe passed back and forth between us. It is exchanged at lightning speed with little or no time spent doing the math. Even Vern, an interested but uninvolved observer of the event, said later he wasn't able to count the exchanges, because they occurred faster than the eye could follow. In terms of entertainment, Vern observed, he thought the performance would have been greatly enhanced by less sleight of hand.

Finally, one of us, either Kenny or me, comes to his senses and throws the stovepipe onto the floor. Neither of us, amazingly, receives a single burn from our encounter with the stovepipe. Ironically, a bit of frostbite does result. That occurs when two enraged naked guys chase a mirthfully squealing little fat kid up the side of a mountain in the middle of a blizzard.

SCENE: It's our first real camping trip. We're all about twelve years old, except for Norm, who's about ten. We've hiked a couple of miles back into the mountains and set up camp alongside a little creek. As usual, we're all wet and cold because Norm jumped off a log at the wrong time and dumped the rest of us into the creek. We take off our boots and are drying them next to the fire, having learned earlier in our lives not to dry wet boots next to a fire while they're still on your feet. Norm glances down and notices that Kenny's brand-new boots are starting to smoke.

"I'll save them," he shouts.

"Noooo!" shouts Kenny.

Norm snatches up the boots and thrusts them into the icy stream.

"Hunh!" he exclaims. "Now that's interesting. Both toes popped right off your boots, Kenny."

Vern and I start supper while Kenny chases the little fat kid up the side of the mountain.

SCENE: Norm and I go to see *The Thing*, the most terrifying movie of the time even though it wouldn't raise a single goose bump on one of today's hardened audiences. We're into our later teens by now, but we're still shaken up by *The Thing*. We get in my car and start to drive home. Then we hear something dragging under the car.

"I wonder what that could be," I say.

"Maybe it's a body," Norm says, always quick to escalate a simple event to crisis proportions.

"It's not a body," I say.

Neither of us wants to stop and see what is dragging under the car. We're both still thinking about *The Thing*.

I pull up to Norm's drive and stop in the middle of the road. Norm's house is about a hundred yards away in the daytime, a half mile at night. As he gets out, I say casually, "Check under the car and see what's dragging."

Norm squats down and looks under the car.

"Holy bleep!" he says. "I see something with two arms!"

I think he must be joking. In case he isn't, though, I press the gas pedal to the floor and let out on the clutch. The car jumps twenty feet through the air. After that, I don't hear the dragging anymore. I have shaken the thing, or perhaps The Thing, loose.

Norm is still squatted down looking under the car when it lunges ahead. The Thing flies out into the middle of the road and stands straight up. It is flapping two arms!

On his way into the house Norm banks high up on the side of the Nelson woodshed, ricochets off the apple tree, almost spins out on the slick grass, but now has a straight shot at the back door.

Norm's dog, Prince, is asleep on the back porch. Prince has no reason to expect Norm to be outside in the dark. He leaps up, trying to growl, but he has momentarily swallowed his tongue. "Urraaah!" goes Prince. "Urraaah!" just happens to be the sound The Thing made in the movie. Norm collides full length with his dog. They crash through into the kitchen. The biting is horrendous! Norm says later it took him two weeks to brush the taste of dog off his teeth. His mother grounds him for teasing Prince and getting his clothes ripped to shreds. The next day Norm discovers that The Thing is an old army overcoat.

I was still studying Norman now as he guided the boat up the river. How, I asked myself, could a man be so different from the boy, a boy who routinely turned the simplest event into a catastrophe. Norm started to smile.

"What are you smiling at?" I asked.

"I was just thinking of the time you tried to split one of the camp biscuits you baked. You hit it with a hatchet and the biscuit shot out from under the blade and wasn't even scarred!"

He started roaring with laughter over this gross exaggeration of my biscuit. (It was, too, scarred!) Norm's eyes filled with tears of mirth. As he felt blindly for his handkerchief, he accidentally knocked over his rod. He jumped up to grab it and stepped on the rod. It snapped in half. "I broke my brand-new rod!" he yelped.

"Steer the boat!" I shouted. "Steer the boat!"

Moments later the two of us were over the side and out in the icy river pushing the boat through inch-deep water flowing over a gravel bar. The water suddenly deepened, and the boat began to float and drift away. We each made a desperate leap and grabbed the side of it. As the boat drifted off downriver, we each managed to hook a leg up over the gunnel, but couldn't quite make it the rest of the way into the boat. We floated along in this fashion for some time, the boat turning this way and that. Presently we came to a group of men fishing from the shore. They regarded us somberly.

"How you doing?" Norm asked them pleasantly, casually, as if this was our normal means of operating a boat.

"Fair to middlin'," one of them responded. "How about you fellas?"

"About the usual," Norm said, his voice starting to quiver from the strain of hanging on to the gunnel.

Silently, the shore fishermen watched as we drifted off down the river.

"They seemed impressed!" Norm grunted.

"Yeah," I grunted back. "This might catch on. Before long maybe everyone will be fishing this way."

"I don't know how we managed to end up in this predicament," Norm said.

In that moment I felt forty years younger. "It's not so bad," I told him. "Actually, it feels just like old times."

Comments I
Could Do Without

O ver the years I've accumulated a variety of comments I'd just as soon not hear from my outdoor associates, or others, for that matter. In the belief that these comments might be instructive to the general population, I have presented a few of them here. A certain amount of outdoor experience on the part of the reader may be required for proper interpretation of each comment. I would supply the interpretation myself, except I am tired and cranky and don't see why I should have to do all the work here. If you had spent half the night walking out of the mountains on a dark and creepy road, you would be tired and cranky, too, and I doubt you would have any difficulty interpreting the first comment.

"Holy bleep! Is that gas gauge *right*?"

Here are some other comments I could do without.

"Now this is what I call being prepared, Pat. You carry an extra drain plug for your boat right up here next to the fish finder."

"Just drop your rod in the water and we'll ease out of here real quiet like, 'cause I've guided in this swamp nigh on to forty years and ain't never seen nothin' like that there before."

"The only way we'll get that out of Pat is to push it the rest of the way through his ear and cut off the barb."

"I sure wouldn't have eaten that third helping of chili if I'd known I was gonna be squeezed into a truck cab with you two fellows for the rest of the night."

"Well, it seemed like a good idea at the time."

"Remember, don't look down and you'll be all right."

"Hey, weird! Where did that rock come from? You don't normally see them up this high." —Alaskan Bush Pilot

"Watch this!" —A comment often made by someone just prior to his spending the next three months in a full-body cast

"Hold on real tight, 'cause I ain't never tried this before." —A comment made by someone just prior to both of us spending the next three months in full-body casts

"Whazzat?"

"Of course I got us permission to fish here. Now shut up and crouch down behind this bush till that truck goes by."

"Sure the fishing's great here, Unk—this stream's been closed all year." —My nephew Shaun, age ten

"Gun it when you hit the steep, narrow part or that ol' bike'll mess you up something awful." —Dave Lisaius, hunting partner

"Didn't you hear me tell you to gun it?" —Dave Lisaius

"Well, we didn't get all the mess sopped up in the back of the SUV. But what the heck, this is Wyoming. The car rental company will understand." —Jim Zumbo, hunting editor

"Naw, the name don't mean nothin'. Now if one of you boys will bite down on Ol' Thunder's ear, I'll throw a saddle on him for Pat." —Hunting outfitter

"We're way overloaded, but I'm a good ninety percent sure we can clear that ridge." —Alaskan Bush Pilot

"Naw, you can't be in quicksand, Pat. But just in case, hand me the worm can." —Vern Schulze, fishing pal, age twelve

"Run!"

"Duck!"

"Jump!"

"Hide!"

"Just for the heck of it, let's everybody slip into a life pre-server."

"Now this ain't gonna hurt one bit, son. It's just I always like to put in my earplugs, so I can concentrate better."

"Oh-oh, here comes your wife [your mom, the game warden, the cops, somebody, something]."

"Quick, tell me again, which bear has the hump on its back?"

"Okay, everybody be cool now, okay? 'Cause just for the heck of it I'm gonna fire three quick shots up in the air, okay?" —Hunting guide

"Hey, I don't like this at all. The sun ain't supposed to go down over there." —Hunting guide

"Yep, I reckon we shoulda thought to mark our trail on the way in. So I hope one of you fellas either knows some real good woodcraft or thought to bring a cell phone." —Hunting guide

"Just sit back and relax, son. Ain't no sense in both of us being terrified."—Fish and Game helicopter pilot, 1962

"Too small to land in? Son, until I put the chopper down in that clearing, there wasn't any clearing there at all!" —Fish and Game helicopter pilot, 1962

"I don't care if she is climbing the chute, there's no way in hell that elk can bust out of . . . *RUN!*" —Fish and Game elk trapper

"I make it through these rapids one more time, I'm going back to law school." —River guide

"Throw out the anchor! Throw out the anchor!"

"All right, I've had enough! I want each of you boys to come up here one by one and empty your pockets out on my desk." —Miss Swaghart, third-grade teacher

"And guess what, Pat. You get to be test pilot! Don't that

sound fun?" —Crazy Eddie Muldoon, age eight, aeronautical engineer

"And guess what, Pat. You get to test the deep-sea-diving outfit! Don't that sound fun?" —Captain Crazy Eddie Muldoon, age eight

"You kidding me? They actually arrest people for that?" —Montana hunting guide

"Stand back and I'll show you how to really start a campfire."

"Oh-oh. What are your feelings about ghosts [Sasquatches, witches, werewolves, space aliens, men with plastic pocket pen holders]?"

"Shucks, push comes to shove, Pat can bunk with ol' Psycho Mulligan."

"You know that grungy old fishing vest of yours? Guess what I did! It's so cute!" —Wife, Bun

"Say, Grampa, what do you suppose might make an outboard motor, nobody's in particular, go *ta-wahka-ta-wahka-ta-wahka*?"

"Wait a minute. If this is the stew, what happened to the sturgeon bait?"

Well, that's all the comments I've got time for. Now, I need to go get a new gas gauge. As Slim, my mechanic, commented, the gas gauge itself costs only $3.95, but to replace it he first has to disassemble the whole car into pieces no larger than a pocket watch. And so then I commented . . . !

Leakage

When my old friends Vern and Gisela Schulze stopped by for a visit the other day, Vern and I got to regaling our spouses with tales of our youth. We laughed ourselves limp. The ladies, on the other hand . . . Well, maybe they had to have been there.

Here's the interesting thing, though. For the first time, I noticed that Vern is getting along in years. It's not a matter of appearance. As a matter of fact, Vern doesn't look much different than he did at twenty-two, when his hair suddenly turned white. It wasn't my fault, his hair turning white, despite what you might hear from Vern. I thought it might have been that incident with the bear but his mother told me it's a family trait. The bear might have hastened the process, though.

What alerted me to the fact that age is starting to take a toll on Vern is the leakage. It's a common thing in older men, leakage. They'll start telling one of their favorite stories and suddenly an actual truth leaks out. And that's what Vern did. I was startled at first, and then amazed. In the three hundred or so times I'd heard Vern's version of the story about the bear, I had never once heard this bit of truth.

Although I have written about the incident with the bear before, I know now that I didn't get it right. In all of my writings, I strive to present the unadorned truth. So you can see why, upon hearing Vern leak a major truth, I would be disturbed, knowing that what I had written before about the bear was little more than a lie, a lie Vern had beguiled me into innocently and unknowingly concocting.

I must mention here that Vern has a well-deserved reputation for approaching almost any predicament with calm deliberation. He drives me crazy. Confronted with an impending crisis, I want a companion who doesn't stand around pondering possible solutions. I want a person who ponders nothing but cuts right to the basic question: Does this situation require a panic or not? Particularly if there's going to be a group panic, I want an early start, so as not to get jammed up in the pack. On the other hand, there's nothing more embarrassing than executing an F-BLP—the classic Full-Bore Linear Panic—only to discover that your partner is a mile behind you, still pondering. Anytime I commit an F-BLP I want my partner to join in, out of simple courtesy if nothing else. The only thing I ask is that he not be faster than I am.

But Vern's thing is calm deliberation. "Let's see now," he'll say. "If we don't get a fire going we most likely will freeze to death within the next twenty minutes. Hmmm. What is our best course of action? Ah yes. The very next thing we must do is to find some dry tinder and after that . . ."

Despite my high regard for panic as a response to crisis, I find Vern to have a calming influence on me. Even when we were nine or ten and venturing out by ourselves for the first time into the unknown wilderness—otherwise known as a woodlot behind Vern's house—Vern already greeted the unexpected with calm self-assurance. More than once I yelled at him, "We better head for home, Vern, it's starting to get dark!" He would ponder this a moment and then reply, "But that's what usually happens on camping trips."

In the thousand or so crises Vern and I have encountered together over the past, um, some years, I recall few that aroused Vern to any degree of excitement. Indeed, his usual companions interpreted any expression of concern by Vern as practically a screech of alarm:

"Hmmm," Vern might say. "I don't like the looks of this."

"Holy cow!" a guy cries out. "Why's Vern so excited?"

"It means we're all gonna die!" I yell. "Run for your lives!"

Vern's reputation for calm, deliberate response to crisis is well established among his friends and associates. But did he acquire it honestly or by clever manipulation of our own imaginations? That is the question I will address here, beginning with a brief summary of my report on the bear as previously written.

Vern and I were in our early twenties and on our first elk hunt. The country we hunted was impossibly steep and treacherous or, in other words, typical elk habitat. To make matters worse, as was our tendency, we somehow managed to enmesh ourselves in near-impenetrable brush slightly higher than our heads. I soon lost track of Vern, who had angled off to my left and higher up the mountain. Occasionally we'd exchange whistles to establish our locations. As I struggled through the brush, my whistle became reduced to a *whsssssss*. Vern's remained sharp and clear. That's because he had found a trail providing him easy passage through the brush. As he moseyed along, the thought occurred to him, as he claimed later, that he might invite me to join him on the trail. Chuckling softly at this ridiculous notion, he congratulated himself on the good fortune of having someone down in the brush to flush game in his direction. And soon some game was flushed.

Something large crashed though the brush up ahead of me. The creature obviously could hear me, and occasionally it would leap up to peer over the brush, trying to get a fix on my location. I would jump, too, trying to get a glimpse of it. Finally, we jumped simultaneously, and there we were, the creature and I, for a split second, peering at each other. I actually glimpsed only a flash of black. Black? Since I had never before seen an elk, let alone hunted one, I assumed what I saw could be an elk. Who knew, maybe there were such things as black elk.

The creature did not share my confusion. It knew exactly what I was, and now, where I was. With considerable racket, it turned and started crashing up the steep slope. Suddenly, a shot rang out, followed instantly by another shot. Because it was virtually impossible to fire a bolt action that fast, I assumed there must be another hunter up on the mountain, both of them shooting almost together. I yelled to Vern. "Did you get it?"

"Yeah," he yelled back calmly. "As a matter of fact, it's practically on top of me."

"Who else shot?"

"Nobody. I missed with the first shot and hit it with the second."

Notice here the use of the word "missed."

I finally worked my way up out of the brush. Vern was standing next to a large dead bear.

"Wow!" I gasped. "I can't believe this. You mean you've been on a trail all this time?"

"Yep, I missed him clean with that first shot," Vern repeated.

"Lucky thing you got him with the second, though," I said. "Looks like the bear was about ready to take you out. I guess it hit the trail over there and bore right in on you."

"It was almost on top of me when I shot," Vern said calmly. "Naturally I had to react pretty fast after missing that first shot."

"Fast is right!" I said.

Notice once again Vern's repetition of the words "missed"

and "missing." Notice also how he lets me fill in the blanks with my imagination. In my imagination I can see the bear bursting onto the trail scarcely a hundred feet away and zeroing in on Vern. At fifty feet, Vern snaps off a shot. Misses! With lightning reflexes, he slams in another round and fires at point-blank range. The bear drops at his feet! Vern remains his usual calm self.

I shake my head in amazement. "So you were on a trail all this time and didn't tell me!"

We now take a sizable chunk out of a century and jump ahead to Vern and Gisela's visit. We are sitting in our living room as Vern and I recount the story of his first bear. Our wives show no visible signs of life, but Vern and I are thoroughly enjoying ourselves. Vern, wheezing from laughter, usually takes the story up to the point where he says, "I could hear something crashing through the brush and headed in my direction." At this point, he would pause, as if to recollect a detail or perhaps catch his breath. That was my signal to jump in.

"That bear hits the trail going flat-out and headed right for Vern, and Vern snaps off the fastest two shots from a bolt-action rifle I've ever heard," etc. Vern would nod in agreement, wiping tears of mirth from his eyes, subtly acknowledging the version of the event I had patched together.

This time, though, Vern doesn't pause but barrels on without interruption. And that's when the leakage occurs. After all this time, Vern, apparently as a result of his present advanced age—he is now much older than I—lets a truth leak out!

I'm startled. I've been sitting here, listening to the well-polished lines, chuckling over them, saying them silently in my head even before Vern speaks them, when the divergence occurs:

"So Pat yells, 'It's headed your way, Vern!' And I can hear it coming up through the brush. Naturally, I think it's an elk, so I'm scanning the brush at about elk-head high, expecting it to come blasting out of the brush at any second. I slip the safety off my bolt-action thirty-ought-six and rest the butt of the rifle in the crook of my right arm, the barrel pointing straight up, my finger on the trigger . . ."

What's this? I think. *Rifle in the crook of his arm? Pointed straight up? I've never heard this before.*

Vern continues: ". . . and then suddenly everything goes real quiet and I think the elk must have stopped. I look this way and that, but no elk. Then I hear kind of a grunt. I look down. A large bear is standing next to me! I snap off a quick shot . . . straight up in the air!"

Well, there you have it—"straight up in the air." Imagine, if you will, what at age twenty-two this confession, this leakage of the truth, would have done to Vern's reputation for calm, deliberate action. He would never have lived it down. But notice also that Vern did not resort to crude lying, as most of us would have done. "I *missed* with the first shot," he had told me, only neglecting to mention over all these years that the miss had been by ninety degrees!

It was about the most cunning and reprehensible and disgusting deception I've ever known one outdoorsman to pull on another. So I've been thinking of using it myself.

The Last Honest Man

It's odd. You can pal around with somebody for years, trust him with your most secret of secrets, use his stuff, play practical jokes on him, rib him good naturedly about his receding hairline, borrow money from him, all the things you expect out of a healthy and mutually rewarding friendship, and then one day you take him fishing. That's when you discover in him this monumental flaw. Such was the case with my old buddy Parker Whitney.

Parker is rich, but I don't hold that against him. It isn't his fault. He inherited the money and therefore didn't have to fritter away his life earning it himself. He's a very nice guy, always cheerful and upbeat and optimistic, which is not only highly irritating but also what happens when you don't have to go out and grub for money. It has been my experience and observation that grubbing for money makes people grumpy.

Why Parker would want to hang out with a couple of

grumpy guys like Retch Sweeney and me I have no idea. Maybe it's the sense of adventure. Until he met us, Parker lived a rather sedate—by which I mean boring—life, piddling away his time at the Yacht Club, the Country Club, the Players Club, and the like. But no more. Since he began hanging out with Retch and me, he seems suspended in an almost continuous state of excitement, even going so far as to shout out in his sleep, "Stop, you fools, you'll get us all killed!" That at least is what his wife, Jane, tells us. Jane also thinks Retch and I take advantage of her husband.

"You two are dreadful," she told us the other day while we were waiting for Parker to throw together his gear for a fishing trip. "Why on earth would you send Parker into thick brush to drive out that huge bear?"

"Why, to get the bear to come out of the brush, so Pat and I could shoot it," Retch explained. "We wouldn't send him into the brush if we didn't have a good reason. It could be dangerous, particularly when you don't shoot any better than Parker does."

"Yeah," I said. "And then Parker ruined it. He stayed so close to the bear when they came out of the brush that neither Retch nor I wanted to risk a shot. Listen, Jane, we really do look out for Parker."

"Good grief, you mean he was that close behind the bear?" Jane gasped.

"Actually, he was in front of the bear," Retch said before I could stop him. "That husband of yours has got some dandy moves, I can tell you that, Jane. I guess when you're a rotten shot, you have to develop some pretty darn good moves."

About then Parker came down the stairs all packed and ready to go. "Hi, guys!"

"Geez, Park, we're only going for a couple of days," Retch said. "You look like you got enough stuff there for a month."

"Most of it is first-aid supplies. Ha! Only joking, Jane, only joking. We're just going fly-fishing, right fellows? Nothing dangerous about that, is there?

Retch and I both laughed, shaking our heads. Dangerous fly-fishing! What a card!

Parker gave Jane a peck on the cheek. "Be back Thursday, dear."

"I hope so. Do be alert at all times, Parker."

"Oh, you don't have to worry about that. Besides, I've got Pat and Retch along to watch my back."

"That's so reassuring, dear."

Three hours later we pulled into the headwaters of Deadman's Creek, a stream that remains virtually untouched by other fishermen, not because it has anything to do with a dead man but because the road is a bit rough in spots.

"There, Parker, that wasn't so bad, was it?" I said. "Uh, Parker, did you hear me? We've made it to camp. You can let go of the steering wheel."

"Hey, look at the bright side, Park," Retch said. "You've been wanting to get a new fishing vehicle anyway. Now you've got a great excuse."

I whispered to Retch. "Let's build a fire and set up camp. That'll give Parker time to relax his grip on the steering wheel."

"Good idea," Retch whispered back. "Besides, I don't like looking at that expression on his face. He doesn't even blink. It's creepy."

"Parker did love that truck, though."

"He sure did. Well, at least he's still got the steering wheel to remember it by."

Some people might think Parker's behavior and careless driving inexcusable, but not Retch and I. Our policy is to forgive and forget. We even laughed off the prospect of the long walk out of the mountains at the end of the fishing trip. When Parker got back to town, he could easily arrange to have someone come pick us up. Shoot, as Retch said, he might even send a helicopter, because that's just the kind of guy Parker is—a rich one.

Little did Retch and I realize at that moment that nestled

like a time bomb deep within Parker's character was a monumental flaw about to detonate and destroy the entire trip for us.

By the next morning, Parker was back to his usual cheerful self. We got up early and spread out along the stream and fished for a couple of hours, meeting back at camp for a late breakfast.

"How'd you guys do?" Parker asked.

"Not that great," Retch said. "I caught half a dozen two- and three-pounders, nothing big. I'll make up for it this afternoon, though."

"I'm sure you will," I said. "As for me, I did manage to land a nice five-pounder."

"One of mine may have gone five pounds," Retch said. "Maybe even five and a half."

"Mine was a beaut," I said. "A chunky old fellow. Might have gone six. Put up one heck of a fight. How'd you do, Parker?"

"My goodness, after hearing what you guys caught I'm embarrassed to say. I only caught half a dozen and not a one was over ten inches."

Any experienced angler would have recoiled in shock at that pitiful admission. Parker Whitney single-handedly had just wiped out at least three hundred years of angling tradition.

He had blurted out a bald-faced truth!

"Wait! Stop!" I exclaimed. "Let me see if I understand this. There were witnesses present when you caught those fish, right, Parker? Witnesses who might show up and testify against you?"

"No, I don't think so. I didn't see anyone."

I looked at Retch. He shook his head in disbelief.

"Parker," I said, "do you know why catch-and-release fishing was invented?"

"Certainly. To conserve fish populations."

"That, too," I said. "But the real reason for catch-and-release is . . . Oh, just let it go, Parker. Once you've had a little more experience and have grasped some of the finer points of fly-fishing, you'll be better prepared for the, uh, truth about catch-and-release. Right now you couldn't stand the truth!"

"What?" Retch said. "What's going on?"

I took him aside and explained what we had to do. Retch didn't take it well.

"I don't see why that affects you and me," he whined, wiping his cheek with the back of his hand. "Parker's taking all the fun out of catch-and-release."

"The point is, Retch, we all have to play by the same rules. At this stage of his development, Parker is incapable of understanding the rules."

The next time when we came in from fishing, Parker asked how we did.

"I caught two small ones and a nine-incher," I confessed. "How about you, Retch?"

"Caught four," he said. "The biggest was a fif . . . a fif . . . a ten-incher."

It was the worst catch-and-release fishing Retch and I had done in twenty years.

Then a strange thing happened. On the final day of our fishing trip, I caught and released a dozen fish that I bet would have gone better than two pounds. I'm not sure what they might have weighed separately. Retch didn't do any better.

"Where's Parker?" I asked. "He should be back by now."
"Oh, he went way off down in the canyon. Last I saw of him he was going around that sharp bend."

Parker didn't get back to camp until almost dark. And what an amazing tale he had to tell. He said he had found some deep pools far down in the canyon and had pulled out one huge trout after another. He said it was like the fish had never seen an artificial fly before. He said they were absolutely savage. He said he was still shaky all over from the thrill of it.

"Well, Parker," I said, "I was going to explain to you the true reason for catch-and-release, but maybe you've already hit upon it."

"Indeed?" Parker replied. "You really think so?"

"Yes, indeed," I said. "I think you may even have mastered the art."

"Gee, thanks. Of course, I knew you guys would believe me, but there are a lot of my friends who'd think I was just telling fish stories. So after I got some of the larger fish in the net, I videotaped them."

"You videotaped them? Hmm. Well, I may have to do some more work on your basic technique, Parker. Tell me, what fly were you using?"

The next day we drew straws—it makes me laugh just thinking about it—to see which of the three of us would hoof it out of the mountains and send someone back for the other two. Parker lost. He immediately took off at a brisk walk down the road.

"Remember the helicopter!" Retch shouted after him.

Parker waved back.

"Was that a wave?" Retch said.

"I think it was," I said. "It looked kind of like a wave."

Sometime later Retch and I were sitting around the campfire roasting our last wiener when the conversation turned to the flaw in Parker's character.

"You don't suppose Parker tricked us, do you?" Retch said. "Like he fakes us into telling the truth about catch-and-release, then he pulls a switch on us and comes up with the big fish story?"

"Naw," I said. "He was telling the truth. I just don't know what to do about him. Parker really is the last honest man. For example, if he tells us he's sending a helicopter for us, he's sending a helicopter for us. That's all there is to it. Parker just has that flaw in his character. It's impossible for him to lie."

"You think he'll ever change, if we continue to set the right example for him?"

"Not a chance. He's hopeless, I'm afraid."

"You hear a helicopter?"

"Naw. You?"

"Naw."

"How long's it been now, since Parker left?"

"Just a little over a week. Why do you ask?"

"No reason."

Pockets

As Bun and I were walking out of a restaurant the other night, I suddenly stopped.

"What now?" Bun asked.

"Just looking for my car keys," I explained.

"Maybe you left them in the car," she said hopefully.

"If I did," I said, "the car would be halfway to a chop shop in Seattle by now. As you can see, it's still sitting where we left it. No, I put the keys in one of my pockets."

"Good grief!" Bun cried. "This is worse than I thought! We'll freeze to death before you find them."

She was exaggerating, of course, but only to call attention to my affinity for pockets. Pockets are practically a hobby of mine. Or maybe a love affair. Normally attired on a winter evening out, I'm equipped with approximately twenty pockets: four in my slacks, two in my shirt, five in my "Adventurer's" sports jacket, which includes a secret compartment for stashing my passport, another sneaky little zippered chamber for emergency cash, and another larger secret pocket intended for what I know not, except possibly smuggling. Then there is my sporty top coat, which has pockets inside of pockets, pockets for warming hands, pockets for storage, pockets for display and pockets for secrets, pockets that zip, pockets that button, pockets that tie, pockets that stick, pockets that gape, pockets with secret passages into other pockets, and pockets with pockets.

Although Bun thinks twenty an absurd number of pockets required for dinner out and a movie, I find it barely adequate. Suppose there's an emergency of some sort on our way home from the movie, an earthquake, say, or another eruption by Mount St. Helens, and we're trapped out in the open miles from home. I figure the two of us could survive for at least two weeks on the contents of my pockets.

What do I carry in my pockets for an evening out? Well, let's see what we have here: keys, display handkerchief, working handkerchief, billfold, checkbook, notepad, coin purse, nail clippers, pocketknife, breath mints, aspirin, anti-acid packets, empty anti-acid packets (don't litter!), leftover crackers, breadsticks, and candies from restaurant (although not the most recent), pipe, pipe cleaners, pipe tool, pipe lighter, tobacco pouch, pocket watch, pen, penlight, reading glasses, theater ticket stubs for past year, a mysterious matchbook with the name "Tootsie" and a phone number scratched on the cover (better not call that one!), swizzle stick collection, assorted toothpicks, two letters and three postcards I must remember to mail before next postage hike, three punch cards for free video movies, each short two punches, and, finally, a dried-up twig cut from a tree I meant to identify in my tree field book, which for some reason isn't in one of my pockets.

All right, twenty pockets is an adequate number for an evening out. For hunting, on the other hand, I need a lot more pockets. I won't go into the hunting items in my pockets, except to say that I am always hunting for them. Take, for example, the little wrench you use to change the screw-in choke tubes for your shotgun. By the time I find it, the birds I'm after have gone south for the winter. Even though I have a vast array of shell loops to keep my shells neatly lined up in double rows across my hunting vest, I somehow always end up carrying the shells in my pockets. Why is that? I suppose it's because I'm in too much of a rush to get to the business at hand. It's simply much easier to dump a box of shells into my pockets and be on my way rather than to stand around inserting shell after shell into individual loops. Certain pockets, by the way, should be reserved for shells only. Otherwise, keep in mind that your attempt to chamber a roll of breath mints can always be passed off as a bit of clowning around.

No matter what pockets you may share and be acquainted with in your day-to-day life, you have not truly experienced pockethood until you get into backpacking. The average backpacker is a walking tower of pockets. His pants alone could supply a family of eight with all the pockets they'd need for a year. Any piece of fabric on a backpacker either contains a pocket or is no farther than an inch away from a pocket. Lost backpackers have starved while frantically searching for the pocket in which they stashed an energy bar. (Well, maybe not. Could happen, though.)

Here is one of the strange pocket phenomena I observed during my days of serious backpacking. I would start out on a trek with pockets empty and the pack crammed full. Bit by bit over the course of several days the contents of the pack would migrate from the pack to my pockets. I would return with my pockets bulging and the pack practically empty, except maybe for sleeping bag and tent. I'd be so lumpy other backpackers would assume I suffered from some mysterious and exotic disease: "Way to go, man! Don't let it hold you back!"

The modern fishing vest is perhaps the pinnacle of pocketdom. I have pockets in my fishing vest I haven't visited in years. Some, I'm afraid to go into. For a while last summer, one of the pockets seemed to be showing signs of life, although probably nothing of any great intelligence.

When I was a kid, I didn't have a fishing vest but had to make do with my pants and shirt pockets. My friend Vern and I occasionally shared a bait can. If I wanted to go off in a different direction, I sometimes would take three or four backup worms and, lacking any other container, drop them in my shirt pocket. This means of transporting worms came to a sudden halt one wash day when my mother was sorting out clothes and emptying pockets. When I saw her holding my shirt, I thought she had taken up some kind of folk dancing. She appeared to be singing, too, but I couldn't hear the words. Just as well. By the time I rescued them, the worms were pretty much shot. But then again, so was my mother.

Mostly what we carried in our pockets as kids were throwing rocks. Whenever you saw a good throwing rock, you picked it up and put it in your pocket. But you never threw the rocks in your pocket, because they were special. If you had the need to throw a rock, you picked up any old ordinary rock. So by the end of any day that you spent afield, your pockets would be filled with rocks. You would be only four-foot-three but tip the scales at upward of two hundred pounds. Once when I was walking through the woods at dusk a large black stump leaped up behind some bushes and chased me for a good half mile. I personally had no trouble outrunning the stump, but it was starting to gain on my pants.

I find it hard to imagine how people could survive without pockets. You'd be walking around all the time with your hands crammed full of stuff. Cavemen, of course, didn't have pockets. So how did they carry all their stuff, like hankies for example? Now that I think about it, I don't want to know.

Actually, pockets were a fairly late fashion development. Neither the Romans nor the early Greeks had pockets. If Aristotle was so smart, how come he didn't come up with a simple idea like pockets? Makes you wonder, doesn't it? Pockets, in fact, were not invented until the Middle Ages, when they brought about an era of great productivity, largely because people were no longer always standing around with their hands full and could now use them to make things. Believe me, modern life would not be what it is today without the invention of pockets. So maybe the Romans and Greeks were on to something.

As Bun and I stood shivering in the parking lot outside the restaurant while I searched for my keys, she asked, "How many pockets to go?"

"Only about eight," I said.

"Well, look later," she said. "I have a set of keys."

"Where?" I asked.

"In my pocketbook, Lumpy."

Now there was an idea. A pocketbook!

Ralston Comes Through

I don't believe in fortune-telling or any of that other occult stuff, and I certainly don't believe in ghosts, except on occasion, when, say, I'm alone on a dark night in some big old house with creaky floors and the sound of chains being dragged up and down stairs. As far as spirits from "the other side" go, I've seen only one of those, and I do have some doubts about him. His name was Ralston and he had red hair. People tend to scoff when I mention Ralston, but that's only because they don't understand the circumstances in which I encountered him.

When I was a boy of twelve, I hung out a great deal with my cousin Buck, who was about eighteen. Despite the differences in our ages, Buck regarded me not merely as his loyal sidekick but as a royal pain in his very existence. I, on the other hand, regarded Buck as my hero, because at that point in his development he knew everything worth knowing. He told me so himself, so I knew it to be true. Later, as I often mention, Buck turned out to be only slightly smarter than celery. But at eighteen he still knew everything.

Big, loud, handsome, and vain, Buck boasted constantly about his skills as a hunter and fisherman, except when he was ridiculing my own efforts in those activities. "A fish would never bite an ugly thing like that," he'd say, studying a fly I had just tied. "That would never fool a fish. You got to make it look at least a little bit like a real insect, dummy." My self-esteem was not one of Buck's major concerns.

So one day I decided to run a psychological test on Buck, just to determine for myself if my flies looked real, at least to the human eye. I created a huge spider, easily the size of my hand, with wire legs, a big tuft of horsetail hair, and tiny red eyes. I tested it on my mother one morning at breakfast, and you can still see the coffee stains on the ceiling. That spider gave even me the creeps, and I had invented it. My knowledge that Buck harbored an unreasonable fear of spiders was not a matter of coincidence in my choosing this particular pattern. As any research psychologist knows, an experiment should be designed in such a way as to produce discernible results. Even though I had had little psychological training at age twelve, I expected this experiment to produce discernible results. It did.

For all his ridiculing of me, Buck possessed one quality that made up for that particular shortcoming—he owned a car. Not much of a car but a car. And a car was needed for hunting and fishing. After I'd dug worms or caught the grasshoppers, Buck would reluctantly take me fishing with him in his car. This particular summer, however, the fishing was terrible. Every lake and stream had been hammered hard not only by local anglers but hordes of tourists passing through. Buck and I had driven all over three counties looking for decent fishing and found not a single piece of water where the fish weren't practically comatose.

"I give up," Buck said one day.

"You can't give up, Buck," I said. "Sooner or later we'll

find a spot nobody else knows about. We'll find the perfect fishing spot."

"Don't be stupid," Buck said. "We've tried everywhere."

"I've got an idea," I said. "We could go see Mrs. Schlavoknee. She tells fortunes and even talks to spirits and like that. Shoot, Buck, it's worth a try, if for a couple of bucks she and her spirits can tell us where to find fish."

"Mrs. Schlavoknee! You ever see that place of hers? Gives me the creeps just thinking about it. On the other hand, maybe it'd be worth a couple bucks, if she'd aim us at some good fishing. I know some businessmen who won't do a deal without consulting Mrs. Schlavoknee first. So why not consult her on fishing? I'm glad I thought of this."

Early the next morning we knocked on Mrs. Schlavoknee's screen door. The plump, blowsy fortune-teller emerged from the interior shadows. Her reddish-gray hair looked as if it had been the victim of a small explosion. A cigarette dangled from her mouth, which was lavishly smeared with a bright red, rather greasy lipstick.

"What?" she said to Buck.

Buck told her about our fishing problem. They then negotiated a price, which, not surprisingly, just happened to be all the money Buck had on him. Buck had been going to let on he had only fifty cents, but I'd told him he couldn't get away with that, not with a fortune-teller, and I was right.

Mrs. Schlavoknee sat us down at a table in her parlor. It was a sturdy, round table with a tablecloth draped over it. The cloth hung clear to the floor. What I took to be a crystal ball glistened roundly in the middle of the table. The dancing flames of candles sent shadows flickering eerily about the ceiling and walls. I heard something creaking about upstairs, possibly dragging chains. I whispered to Buck. "Let's get the heck out of here!"

"Don't be stupid," he reassured me. "Oh, I forgot. That's not a choice for you."

Still, I could tell that Buck's nerves weren't faring much

better than my own. He glanced this way and that and occasionally at the ceiling, possibly because he heard the sound of chains dragging across the floor.

Mrs. Schlavoknee booted-up her crystal ball but couldn't seem to get it to download anything. Then she said she would have to do a seance and see if she couldn't tune in to her spirit guide, "Ralston," because he was a fishing enthusiast, even if "over on the other side." What kind of fish could they have on the other side, I wondered, little ghost trout and little ghost bass? One thing for sure, fishing on that side had to be a whole lot better than it was on *this* side.

Mrs. Schlavoknee leaned back and shut her eyes and began to moan as if in pain. Then she slumped back in her chair and became deathly still, so much so that a couple of times I thought I detected a snore. The fortune-teller had proven herself not only daffy but boring. I looked around. I yawned. I fidgeted. I jammed my hands into my pockets. I touched something fuzzy. The spider! I glanced at Buck. His hard, peevish eyes glared across the table at Mrs. Schlavoknee. What better time to run the spider test on him! I pulled out the spider and set it on the table next to his elbow. With malice aforethought, I had attached a black thread to the spider, so I could jiggle it along the table on its wire legs.

Just then Mrs. Schlavoknee moaned eerily. "Ralston, is that you?" I returned Buck's smirk: And now we'll hear the spirit talk, I suppose. Yeah, right.

"Yes-s-s-s," quavered a voice seemingly rising out of the crystal ball. "I'm here. I'm very close."

Buck stiffened in his chair. I could feel the springs in my legs winding up, ready to fire me out Mrs. Schlavoknee's door.

Mrs. Schlavoknee moaned on. "Can you tell the boys where they might find some good fishing, Ralston?"

Ralston replied, "Boulder-r-r-r Cri-i-i-ick. Below-w-w the fall-l-ls."

"Thank you, Ralston," Mrs. Schlavoknee said. She sat silently for a few moments and then emerged from her trance. "I hope Ralston gave you some useful information, boys. He's usually quite accurate and . . ." Her eyes widened in unholy horror. What hideous terror from the realms of darkness had she glimpsed, what monstrous evil had she summoned unknowingly out of the depths of unholy darkness! And then I made out what Mrs. Schlavoknee was screeching:

"SPIDER-R-R-R-R!"

I jerked the spider off the table. It landed with a plop on the floor, where I kicked it under the edge of the tablecloth. That's when this really weird thing happened. The table became infused with a life of its own. It went wild. It gave a little jump, then darted about the room like a drop of water on a red-hot skillet, finally coming to rest against a curtained doorway. That's when I noticed something even stranger yet. Well, there was absolutely no doubt now that that table had become the vehicle of a spirit. I tried to point this out to Buck, just to teach him a good lesson. But Buck wasn't there.

Then the springs in my legs let go. I shot out of the house and down the street so fast I caught up with Buck only half a block away. He was surprised to see me so soon, because he was still accelerating.

"Boy, that was scary, hunh, Buck? The way the table darted about the room."

"Table?" Buck gasped. "What are you talking about, dummy? Didn't you see the size of that spider? It was big as a saucer! I could see its fangs getting ready to chomp me. A spider that size ain't nothin to fool around with. It could run you down, if it took a mind to."

"But what about Ralston, Buck?"

"Ralston! Ha! What a fraud that was! There wasn't no Ralston."

"There was, too, because I saw him."

"Oh yeah. What did this Ralston look like then?"

"Well, I only caught a glimpse of him, but I can tell you this—he had red hair."

"Red hair! You are so dumb. Spirits don't have red hair. They don't have hair. Spirits are made out of, out of, uh, nothing! So you can't see them, because you can't see nothing. Understand?"

"Yeah," I said, it never occurring to me that Buck was starting to slip into his celery phase. "Anyway, let's go fishing. Got any idea where we might catch some fish?"

"Hmmm, let's see," he mused. "I think maybe we should try Boulder Crick. Below the falls might be good. We haven't tried that."

"Hey, I was thinking the same thing," I said.

"Sure you were, dummy." Buck flicked a piece of screen off his shoulder. "Cripes," he said. "You ever hear of someone locking a screen door around here?"

It wasn't until the following week that Buck and I made it up to Boulder Creek and found a narrow, winding trail that took us down below the falls. The fishing was fantastic, and nobody but us knew about it. We couldn't believe our luck. We spent the whole day on the creek and saw only one other person. I never got close enough to talk to him, but I did notice he had red hair. It wasn't the sort of thing I wanted to mention to Buck, though.

Trumped by a King

Folks who live along Alaska's Kenai River like to brag that it's the greatest sportfishing river in the world. I can't dispute that. I actually caught a fish there. A big fish! A king salmon! The guide estimated the fish at something over sixty pounds. We hadn't hauled it out of the water yet so ... SIXTY POUNDS! SIXTY SILVERY FLASHING POUNDS OF KING SALMON FURY IN A SINGLE FISH!

The guide wasn't impressed.

"You wanna keep it?" he asked, shrugging dismissively.

Was the man crazy or what? Of course I wanted to keep it! I raged with desire to haul that fish up out of the water and preserve it forever on my office wall.

Visitor: What a beautiful fish! Who caught it?

Me: I caught it, bud. What did you think, I picked it up at a garage sale?

Visitor: Well, pardon me! There is your reputation, you know.

I do have a rumored reputation of having an aura of some kind that makes it not only impossible for me to catch fish but also for anyone else fishing in a two-hundred-mile radius of me to catch fish. It's weird how such a rumor gets started, but there are those who actually believe it. Even eminent psychologist and writer Dr. Paul Quinnett once wrote an article claiming to have personally observed my effect on fish. That just goes to show how even a learned scientist like Quinnett can leap to such an absurd conclusion after a mere few dozen fishing trips with me.

"So," the guide said, frowning down at my gorgeous fish thrashing in the net. "You wanna keep it or what?"

"Naw," I said. "Let it go." I watched the greatest fish of my life disappear into the watery shadows of the Kenai River. Pulling out my handkerchief, I gazed off into the distance. That spectacular Alaskan scenery can actually bring tears to your eyes, if you're a poetic type like me.

Actually, the real reason I released the SIXTY-PLUS-POUND KING SALMON was that I had caught it within fifteen minutes of being on the river my first day of fishing. The rule was that once you caught and kept a king, you had to put up your rod for the day. No more fishing for anything. Had I paid mucho moola for this trip to Alaska to fish the Kenai for only fifteen minutes? No way. Obviously, if I could catch a SIXTY-PLUS-POUND KING SALMON in the first fifteen minutes, I could easily hook a dozen others during the day, some even bigger. I never got another bite.

My friends did, though. They each caught kings ranging from the mid sixties into the high seventies. Each of them has his fish mounted and hanging garishly on a wall of his home or office. I just can't believe the taste of some people. It is just so gauche.

The years passed and I fished the Kenai several more times but usually a week too late or a week too early, but sometimes I nailed it right on the button. I hooked and released a hundred or so fish, but I never caught another king even approaching SIXTY-PLUS POUNDS! Some days we caught what my Alaskan friends consider next to nothing. I would hear angry mutterings drifting in my direction.

"It's a stupid myth!" I'd yell at them.

Then one day last year I got an invitation to the Kenai River Classic, sponsored by the Kenai River Sportfishing Association, Inc. In all modesty I must mention that the classic is a pretty exclusive affair. Opening the mail over lunch one day, I said casually to Bun, "Well, this is interesting. I see I've been invited to a pretty exclusive affair."

"Wait a minute," Bun said. "I thought you said *you* were invited."

"Very funny. Well, I'm sure they had a darn good reason. Look, here's the invitation from Brett Huber, the executive director of the Kenai River Sportfishing Association. Brett says right here I'm one of the celebrities they're inviting to the classic."

It took a moment for Bun to stifle her laughter and wipe the tears from her eyes. "If this Mr. Huber actually thinks you're a celebrity, he probably doesn't know about your reputation in regard to fish."

"I'm sure he doesn't believe that nonsense. Besides, he says right here in the letter that he's been reading my stories since he was a little kid. Gee, he must be terribly young to be an executive director. And to have such excellent taste in fine literature."

"Yeah, right."

My friend Dave Lisaius got to join me as a guest of the classic, even though he isn't a celebrity.

"I wonder how come Dave gets to go," I said to Bun.

"Mr. Huber mentioned something about someone to keep an eye on you."

"You've been talking to Brett Huber?"

"No."

A few weeks later Dave and I were happily ensconced in Ms. Billy Shackleton's Gulls Landing Bed and Breakfast over-

looking the Kenai River. The first morning we were there
Dave walked down to Billy's dock, made a cast or two, and
caught a rainbow approximately the size and shape of a VW
Beetle. It was a good sign. And I had actually been touching a
fishing rod at the time.

We had one problem with Billy. Every morning for breakfast she would serve us sausage, bacon, ham, hash browns,
scrambled eggs, omelets, crepes, oatmeal, assorted cold cere-
als, pancakes, waffles, croissants, toast, cinnamon rolls,
oranges, bananas, apples, coffee, tea, and four different
juices. And we would eat it! Oh, not all of it, of course. Often
we skipped the cold cereal.

The classic's fishing tournament lasted two days. We
fished from six A.M. to noon, with three fishermen in each
boat with a volunteer guide. It was exciting. On all sides of us
classic participants were hauling in kings. Those in my boat,
however . . .

The guide was embarrassed. "I don't know what's wrong,"
he said. "I've never had this happen to me before."

"Don't worry about it," I said. "These things happen.
Often."

Dave made up for my bad luck. He came in sixth in the
tournament. He is so lucky.

Overall, my so-called aura didn't even put a dent in the
tournament. Brett Huber told me the other day it was just an
average year for the Kenai River Classic in terms of numbers
of fish caught. Average on the Kenai, of course, means pretty
darn spectacular just about anywhere else.

One of the side benefits of the classic was that I got to hob-
nob with a bunch of U.S. senators, friends Alaska's Senator
Ted Stevens had invited along. I especially enjoyed the company of Wyoming senator Mike Enzi and his wife, Diana. I
was sure both of them were aware of my reputation, because
I was under suspicion by Wyoming Fish and Game for several times shutting down the fishing and hunting in the whole
state. But they never once mentioned it. Maybe they weren't

even aware of that ruckus in the Cheyenne sports shop. Before I could touch a fly rod in one of the display racks, two cowboys tackled me and dragged me away to a bar. It always amazes me how that silly rumor gets around.

The Kenai River Classic is the brainchild of Senator Stevens. About ten years ago, the senator was trying to think up some way to help preserve Kenai River habitat and promote responsible sportfishing, when he came up with the idea for the classic, a fishing tournament funded entirely by entrance fees and contributions from industry. It has since contributed over $2 million for Kenai River habitat protection. He and Alaska governor Tony Knowles are cochairmen of the annual event and two of its most avid and energetic promoters and participants. Senator Stevens, by the way, holds the record for the tournament, a seventy-one-pound king. I know. There may be hearings. No, really, the senator is a superb fisherman, and if he happens to commit an irony, it certainly isn't his fault.

Before heading for the airport and home, Dave and I took a cruise around Soldotna, the home of the classic. While we were eating lunch in a park, a couple guys came up to us and tried to sell us Rolex watches for twenty bucks apiece. Ha! Obviously, they had no idea of the normal price of Rolexes. Dave and I were reaching for our billfolds when the one guy says, "Only kidding." Seeing our disappointment, they introduced themselves as Ron Walden and Jim Golden, pretty fishy names if you ask me. "Say," says Golden, "some of us guys are putting together a little halibut fishing trip and thought you two might like to come along."

Right away I was suspicious. "Just how little are the halibut?" I asked. I could see Golden and Walden were taken aback. They obviously weren't accustomed to dealing with two sharpies like Dave and me.

"They aren't little, they're big!" said Walden.

"How come your friend here said they were little then?" Dave asked.

"I didn't say they were little!" shouted Golden, his eyes taking on a wild look. "Listen, you want to go halibut fishing or not?"

Think about it. Here are these two wild Alaskan characters, complete strangers, who walk up out of nowhere and invite us to go halibut fishing with them. Is this weird or what?

"Sure," I said.

"Darn right," said Dave. "When do we leave?"

Dave and I simply weren't the kind of guys to pass up a chance to go fishing for halibut, even if they were little. Oh sure, now we are, but that's another story.

A Hunter's Breakfast

Nothing improves a hunt more than starting off with a good breakfast. Several recent examples of the hunter's breakfast leap to mind.

I was snoozing peacefully away when the alarm suddenly jolted me awake, feet churning, arms flailing. Punching off the alarm button, I blinked at the clock—three A.M. What foul trick was this? What fiend had committed this atrocity? Ah yes, no fiend other than myself. Feeling fiendish, I flipped on the light, reached over, and shook Bun, who had clamped a pillow over her head. "You awake?" I asked. This, by the way, is standard operational procedure in preparing for an early morning hunt.

"No," she growled.

"Sorry. I thought maybe the alarm had awakened you."

"It didn't. Now shut up."

"That's odd. The alarm practically gave me heart spasms, and it didn't even awaken you. Hunh. Very interesting. Well,

I suppose there's nothing to do but get up. I hope I haven't disturbed you too much. I'll get dressed as quietly as I can. Did you hear what I said, Bun? Did you hear?"

She removed the pillow from her head and gave me a squinty-eyed look in which I could just barely detect a bit of affection, which also might have been some fuzz stuck to the corner of her upper lip. "Oh all right, I'm awake now," she snapped. "How could I not be? So what would you think about my fixing you a nice hot breakfast of bacon and eggs, a big stack of pancakes, and some good strong coffee while you get dressed?"

My heart leaped up. "I'd love it!"

"I thought you would. Well, I was just curious." She clamped the pillow back over her head.

Always remember that wives can respond viciously to the standard operational procedure, and it must never be attempted by beginners, in either marriage or hunting.

"Okay," I said. "I just didn't want you to feel guilty simply because Honey Sweeney is at this very moment up fixing a delicious breakfast for Retch." Retch is my hunting buddy. He has a nice wife. I won't repeat Bun's response, except to say it contained a couple of words that I doubted were even in Honey Sweeney's vocabulary. Actually, there aren't a whole lot of words of any kind in Honey's vocabulary, but she is cute.

I went down to the kitchen and put on the coffee. It occurred to me that lox and bagel would taste pretty good, with some cream cheese and, oh yeah, a slice of onion sprinkled with capers. Made my mouth water just thinking about it. I opened the bread box. No bagels. Nothing but one stale glazed donut. I checked the refrigerator for lox. No lox. At least we had an onion. Then I rummaged around in the pantry and came up with a tin of sardines. You know, it may not be exactly the same as lox and bagel, but sardines and onion on a stale glazed donut with mustard comes pretty darn close. Try it, you'll like it, particularly the next time you're up fixing your own hunter's breakfast at three in the morning.

I drove over and picked up Sweeney. "Hey, ole buddy," I greeted him. "How you doin' on this bright and early first day of hunting season?"

"Mmppphh."

"My sentiments exactly. Couldn't have expressed them any better myself. So what did you have for breakfast?"

Retch yawned. "Oh, just the usual. Honey got up and fixed me a nice thick slab of ham, a couple of eggs, toast, hash browns with gravy, lots of gravy."

"Liar."

"Ha! I did try the standard operating procedure on Honey, though, and you know what she said?"

He told me.

"Gosh, I didn't think Honey had those words in her vocabulary."

"Yeah, she does. But she only uses them at three o'clock on the morning of the opening day of hunting season."

I nodded thoughtfully. This was a response with which I was familiar. "And what did you fix for your hunter's breakfast?"

"A Coke, cheesecake, and some pickles, with pretzels on the side. What did you have?"

"Sardines and onion on a stale glazed donut."

"Sounds good. I'll have to try it sometime."

We drove over to Bart's place to pick him up. He was standing under a light on the back porch digging into a can of Yappo dog food with a spoon.

"Would you look at that?" I said, shaking my head in disgust.

"That's pretty darn bad," Retch said. "You'd think Bart would know better than that." He rolled down the window and yelled out, "Hey, Bart, don't you know no better than to eat out of the can? Get yourself a plate and eat like a civilized human being!"

"I'm feeding the dog, you idiot!" Bart yelled back.

"Shoot," Retch said to me. "For a moment there I thought ole Bart was on to something. You ever taste Yappo?"

"Sure. You did, too. Remember that grouse hunt up in Canada when we ran low on people food?"

"Oh yeah? You mean those weren't meat-loaf sandwiches?"

After Bart got his gear loaded into the back of the truck, he returned to the house and came out with a large bowl. He slid in next to Retch and began to eat.

"Whatcha eatin' there, Bart?" Retch asked.

"Cold chili over a slab of chocolate cake."

"Yum," said Retch. "Personally, though, I would have heated the chili in the microwave."

"Geez, Sweeney, you have absolutely no culinary aptitude. If you heated the chili, it would melt the frosting!"

Then we started reminiscing about great food we had eaten before our wives started worrying about our cholesterol. "Either of you guys remember gravy?" I asked.

Retch rolled his eyes heavenward. "Gra-a-a-vy! Yes! Yes! Yes! When I was a kid we had gravy at every meal. Biscuits and gravy for breakfast, gravy over hot pork sandwiches for lunch, gravy over mashed potatoes and chicken-fried steak for supper! Mmmmm!"

"Gravy was practically a beverage at our house," Bart said. "But biscuits and gravy was my all-time favorite. I wonder if restaurants even serve biscuits and gravy anymore."

"Only one that I know of," I said. "Girt's Gas 'n' Grub."

"Really?" Bart said. "With sausage chopped up in it?"

"Yep. Spread all over a couple of big puffy baking-powder biscuits."

A tear rolled down Bart's cheek. "You guys will hate me for even suggesting this, on my first hunt with you and all, but I wonder if maybe we could stop by Girt's Gas 'n' Grub for some biscuits and gravy."

Retch and I both laughed.

"You got a lot to learn about hunting, Bart," I said. "Sure, you know how to put together a hunter's breakfast, but there's more to the sport than just that."

"For one thing," Retch said, "you got to be out in the field and in position by the crack of dawn."

"But dawn doesn't crack for another two hours," Bart pointed out. "And you said it's only a twenty-minute drive out to where we're going to hunt."

"Gosh, I don't know, Bart," I said, giving my head a thoughtful scratch. "What do you think, Retch? We have enough time to stop by Girt's Gas 'n' Grub?"

"Why else do we get up at three in the morning?" Retch said.

Just by chance we were at that very moment approaching Girt's Gas 'n' Grub. I slowed down and turned into the parking area. The message on the reader board said, SPECIAL: HUNTER'S BREAKFAST, $2.98!

What that might be was anybody's guess.

"Raisins in the hash? You think I put raisins in the hash, Newton? Yep, that's what they are, raisins. No, they don't have wings! Now stop digging at your food and eat!"

"Well, I'd better go over across the crick and chop some more firewood while you light the lantern again. By the way, and please don't take offense at this, Newton, but I think you look a whole lot better without that scraggly beard."

"Here's another little test of your woodsmanship, Newton. Bet you don't know the way back to camp."

"This ain't no time to be checking to see what side of the tree the moss is growing on, Newton. Moss don't care one iota whether you live or die out here."

"It's not a good idea to suddenly shout out 'Sasquatch!,' Newton, even if there ain't no such thing. When you're lost in the woods, just about anything can set off a panic. You got to remember that, son. One good thing, though, I can see camp from up here in the tree."

"Any fool can pound in tent pegs with a hatchet, Newton, but it takes skill to perform that task with the outdoorsman's basic tool—the flat rock! Let me demonstrate."

"What you saw me perform there, Newton, is known technically as the 'Crouch Hop'! Did you notice how I clasped my flattened thumb between my thighs before bounding about camp? You can make up your own chant, but 'Yi Yi Yi!' is one of my favorites, particularly when ladies and children are present."

"I'm sorry about your head, Newton. I hadn't realized you'd decorated your lucky hunting hat with fur and bear claws. Looked to me like it had sprung out of a tree and latched on to your scalp. So that's when I grabbed up the stick."

"I don't care what miners used to do, Newton, we ain't bringing no canary into the tent. If you're going to be so dang fussy, you can do the cooking."

"Time for you to light the lantern again, Newton. I'll be over across the crick. Oh, I should mention that I think you

As the Ear Is Bent

Persons newly introduced to hunting, fishing, and camping can often learn a great deal from paying close attention to the comments of their more experienced companions, particularly those who have entered into geezerhood. What follows is an example of the kind of geezer comments to which a beginning outdoorsman should be particularly alert, if he is to profit from the wisdom of his more experienced companion.

"Since this is your first camping trip, Newton, I'm gonna let you have the side of the tent with a nice view of the stars."

"Sasquatch? Ain't no such thing as a Sasquatch, Newton. You hear all sorts of weird sounds like that outside a tent at night. You go check it out while I look for my glasses."

"I'll go over there on the other side of the crick and chop some firewood, Newton, while you light my old gas lantern."

"Okay, Newton, here's a little problem I thought up to test your sense of direction. Got any idea where we left the car?"

look a whole lot better without that squirrelly little mustache. You bet!"

"That was a nice punt, Newton. I just wish you'd aimed the lantern toward the crick instead of the tent. Come to think of it, of what use are eyebrows, really? Seems to me a fella is just as well off without 'em."

"You see, Newton, a lean-to made out of sticks and a few cedar boughs can make a nice, comfortable shelter. If you don't figure out where we left the car pretty soon, we might think about putting up a few pictures. Ha! Seriously, though, you think real hard about where we parked the car, because I'm not going to give you the answer."

"You what? You found the car, Newton? Now, wasn't it right where I parked it? So there you go. What have I been telling you? Not to worry when you're out with the Old Geez, huh?"

"You'd like to snack on some raisins while you're driving home? What makes you think we brought along any raisins, Newton?"

"Why thanks for saying that, Newton. It's nice to hear that after this little outing with me, you feel much better equipped to survive your next camping trip."

Curly and Mo

A wise old man once advised me, "Whenever you come across a product that's particularly good, buy two or three of it, because the manufacturer will soon discover how good the thing is and stop making it."

I recalled that bit of sage advice while out on a hike this morning. The recollection no doubt was stirred by the distinct sense that if the soles of my hiking shoes were any thinner, my feet could read Braille through them. After a mere twenty-five years of fine and faithful service, the shoes, I'll call them Curly and Mo, are about ready to be put down. I shall hate to do it. Had only I heeded the old man's advice, two new pair just like Curly and Mo would be waiting in the wing tips, or at least right next to them.

For the past five years or so, I could see the end coming for Curly and Mo, and so I have been on the lookout for a pair just like them. I constantly browse shoe departments for their siblings but to no avail.

Shoe Department Guy: "May I help you, sir?"

Me: "I hope so. I'm looking for a pair of hiking shoes exactly like these."

Shoe Department Guy: "Aaaaiii! Get back! Get back!"

It isn't that I haven't discovered many other excellent hiking shoes, but they now are all so high tech. They are such serious shoes, meant for serious walking, by serious guys. I'd look ridiculous plodding along in shoes like that. People might expect me to climb an Alp or something.

Also, I'm historically and philosophically opposed to buying a pair of shoes that cost more than my first car. Curly and Mo cost about eight dollars. They were on sale at a former war surplus store that was trying to morph into a department store. I didn't put a lot of thought into their purchase. For some reason I've long forgotten, I needed a pair of hiking shoes and I needed them fast. I rushed into the store, grabbed a pair off the rack, and hopped around first on one foot, then the other, while I tried them on for size, slapped my money on the counter, and rushed out. It was only later I discovered that I'd hit upon the perfect pair of hiking shoes, at least for me. They were light and comfortable, as well as modest. They didn't put on airs, like some shoes I could mention, although they eventually started to give off some. They were tough, too. In fact, they outlasted the store where I bought them by a couple of decades.

Curly and Mo can sense danger, too. A couple of summers ago I happened to walk within a dozen yards of a cougar at a kill—not on purpose, mind you—and right away Curly and Mo picked up their pace and carried me away at a nice clip. We hadn't actually seen the cougar but had smelled the kill and heard the hissy snarl. Later, we looked back and saw the cougar swim the river. Curly and Mo were so excited by having come that close to an irate cougar, they hopped up and down until I finally made them stop.

Curly and Mo have always had a nice feel for the planet. "Loose rock!" they report. "Ice! Grab something quick!" Sometimes on a good trail high in the mountains early in the morning with the sun rising through the trees, they start to hum.

The wrong shoes or boots can get you killed in the mountains. I once stepped on a loose log and injured my leg in a fall down a steep slope during a winter deer hunt. That was only the first treachery of the bulky, heavy, high-tech boots I was wearing. They were designed to keep my feet warm as toast even if the entire earth frosted over, which appeared to be imminent at the time of my fall.

After I'd fallen, slid, somersaulted, and ricocheted into the bottom of the canyon, I gathered myself together, at least what parts I could find, and started the long climb back to camp. Sensing I was in trouble and in serious need of every bit of energy I had left, the boots began taking on weight, ten pounds, twenty pounds, fifty pounds. I suspected that the boots, having failed in their first attempt with the fall, were still trying to kill me, this time with exhaustion and hypothermia. I felt as if I had a baby hippo perched on one boot and its mother on the other. Then a sinister chill crept over my body—all except for my feet, which were still warm as toast. As I plodded onward and upward through knee-deep snow, I imagined a search-and-rescue team finding me buried in a drift:

"Looks like ol' Pat's been froze solid for at least nine days. Funny thing is, his feet are still warm as toast!"

I survived, of course, but my point is, Curly and Mo would never have gotten me into such a predicament. Not only would they have warned me of the loose log that led to the fall, they would have had my toes on the brink of frostbite long before exhaustion set in. "Back to the fire, you fool," they'd have shouted. "Back to the fire."

Curly and Mo have traveled with me all over the world, tied up in a plastic sack in my suitcase.

Suspicious Custom Inspector: "Ahh, und vhat do ve haff hier in der plahsteec sahk, eh? Aaiiii! Get bahk! Get bahk!"

I'm very careful not to get them stained. For example,

Curly and Mo have hunted turkeys with me in Georgia, doves in Alabama, geese in Minnesota, grouse in Michigan, deer in Montana, elk in Colorado, chukars in Idaho, pheasants in Oregon, and quail in Washington, and so far they haven't been stained by a single drop of blood. Do I know how to take care of a pair of shoes or what?

I'm not into romanticizing things. If I wanted to romanticize something, it certainly wouldn't be a grungy old pair of shoes. I will say, however, that Curly and Mo have carried me out of many a dark woods and out of even darker moods. They are like Prozac with sole.

A weird thing happened a few days ago. I was in one of my somber and reflective moods that Bun refers to as "pouting around the house." (Boy, if that isn't a phrase that can improve my mood!)

"Hey, Bun, how about making me a sandwich?" I called out. "I think a sandwich might cheer me up."

"Take a hike!" she called back.

Well, I really didn't feel up to a hike, and after a bit I dozed off right there at my desk. When I awoke, I looked down and there nestled up next to my feet were Curly and Mo. Usually, Bun doesn't allow them out of the mud room, but somehow they had sneaked by her and made it all the way to the den on their own. Their little tongues were practically panting, begging to go out. How could I refuse? So we took a hike up the mountain behind the cabin, and darned if it didn't make me feel downright chipper. Too bad Bun isn't as sensitive to my moods as Curly and Mo are.

It occurs to me that one of these days I'll have to put the boys down. I have to steel my mind and heart, have to get myself up for this merciful bit of treachery, much as if I were putting down a faithful old dog who had run out the string of his days. On the other hand, though, maybe I could have Curly and Mo bronzed! What a great idea! I could display them on the fireplace mantle in the living room. "Hey, Bun . . . !"

Survivors of the Far Out

One morning a while back I awoke to find myself in a small hovel on the banks of a large river somewhere in the deep interior of South America. Naturally, I was shocked, as anyone would be. I glanced around. A man sat cross-legged on a rusty cast-iron cot next to mine. It was none other than my friend Hempthorn, wearing only his Jockey shorts and a look of sheer horror. He held a club in his hand.

"What happened?" I said. "How did we get here? We must have been kidnapped by terrorists."

"No," said Hempthorn, his eyes darting about the floor, a spectacle that was not only disconcerting but rather disgusting. "We paid a travel agent thirty million credaros each to arrange a fishing trip for us into the heart of South America."

"Oh," I said, gazing out the doorway at a dismal swamp, my view unobstructed by any evidence of a door. "Are you sure this is the heart? I rather think it might be the—"

"Never mind that," Hempthorn interrupted, verging on panic. "We have a serious problem."

"Does it have anything to do with the fact our travel agent wore a fake beard and mustache and ran his agency out of the trunk of a car in an alley behind a tattoo parlor?"

"Maybe, but he seemed okay at the time," Hempthorn croaked.

"Take it easy," I said. "You're starting to croak."

"I don't think I'm that bad yet," he said. "It's possible though. I may have got snake bit while I was up going to the bathroom in the middle of the night."

"We have a bathroom?"

"It's a euphemism for 'a bush outside.' Anyway, the hovel was pitch black and I couldn't see anything. I hadn't taken more than a couple steps when I felt something creepy-crawly squirming all around my bare feet. Snakes, I thought. I'm surprised my screams didn't wake you."

"I heard screams but I thought they were mine," I said. "Something resembling a five-pound bat had perched on my knee."

"No, the screams were mine," Hempthorn continued. "When I came to my senses, I discovered I was crouched on a window ledge about six feet off the floor. Fortunately, the proprietor of the camp had thoughtfully left the window devoid of any glass or I might have been cut to pieces. So what do you think?"

"We have a window?" I said.

"Yes," he said. "But it's very small and difficult to crouch in."

"I think I know your problem," I said, studying the floor. "You were not stepping on snakes. You didn't get snake bit."

"I didn't? What a relief! I'm going to live! What was it on the floor then?"

"Tiny frogs," I said. "The floor must have been completely carpeted with frogs about the size of a dime." I pointed to the floor. "Look, there are your footprints up to the point where you lifted off. With each step, you squished dozens of little frogs with your bare feet! See? The squished frogs are in the exact shape of the soles of your feet."

"Arhhh! Stop!" cried Hempthorn in anguish. "I squished dozens of frogs with my bare feet! And I'm going to live! Arhh!"

I wasn't so sure about that. Hempthorn immediately stiffened straight out on his cot and began to twitch and shudder all over. I had to twitch and shudder a few times myself, and I hadn't been the one to squish frogs with my bare feet.

Presently, I noticed a terrorist approaching our hovel. He seemed vaguely familiar. I wondered if I hadn't seen his picture somewhere, possibly on a post office wall. I hoped he spoke English. On a previous fishing trip to South America, our guide spoke no English at all, resulting in a certain amount of comical confusion and great amusement on his part, particularly with our use of the words "Stop!" and "Help!"

Our new guide gave me a big smile. "Hey, man, you're gonna rock to the max at our little resort here, it is so cool."

I smiled back, and asked slowly, "You . . . speak . . . English?"

"*Sí, señor*, English, Portuguese, Spanish, Japanese, and some French and German I picked up while getting my MBA."

"You have an MBA and you're guiding fishermen in the swamps of wherever we are?"

"Oh, I am not the guide, *señor*. I am the owner. It is I who have made this fishing resort what it is today."

"A collection of hovels."

"Yes! You are very observant, sir. Can you imagine, when I first purchased the resort it consisted of a four-star luxury hotel."

"Ah ha," I said. "That explains the picture in the brochure."

"Exactly," he said. "We really need to get a new brochure out so that it will show the true character of our little resort—the ideal fishing camp! That is what our architects have striven for."

"I suspect they exceeded all expectations," I said.

"Yes," he said. "We are very pleased with the result. It was terribly expensive transforming the four-star hotel into these hovels but well worth it. You can't imagine how disappointed our guests used to be when they stepped off the helicopter seeking adventure and discovered nothing but another luxury hotel."

"Helicopter," I said. "Your guests used to be dropped off by helicopter?"

"I'm sorry to say that is true. Fortunately, at great effort and expense I managed to locate in a farmer's pasture a 1934 bus without springs or padded seats or windows that open to convey our present guests from the airport the four hundred miles through the steaming heat of the swamp to the camp. Perhaps you noticed on your ride in that the bus has been altered in such a manner as to pump large amounts of exhaust directly into the passenger compartment. A nice quaint touch, what?"

"Indeed it is," I said. "I wouldn't have thought of it myself in a thousand years. By the way, when do we start fishing?"

In practically less time than it takes to shout "Stop!" or "Help!" we were roaring up the river in a slender canoe powered by what appeared to be the entire power train from a large and exceedingly fast automobile. Our guide, an amiable young maniac, thoughtfully turned up the volume on his boom box to drown out both the thundering of the engine and the screams of Hempthorn, which I appreciated.

The fishing turned out to be quite good, and we landed numerous very nice fish heads. We would have preferred to land the whole fish but, as is sometimes the case in South America, the water teemed with piranha. As soon as a fish was hooked and started to thrash about, the piranha attacked it. Hempthorn and I soon tired of the catch-and-release of fish heads and decided to try fly-fishing for the piranha themselves, which made the guide nervous because he apparently thought he was trapped in a canoe with two crazy persons.

Soon we were hooking piranha right and left on flies. Almost any streamer worked fine, but the most productive imitated a human finger. The piranha, not surprisingly, showed no favoritism to one of their own, and once again we landed mostly heads. Oddly, the few whole piranha we landed thrashed madly about until they were in the bottom of the canoe, at which point they lay perfectly still and seemed totally content with their situation. I figured they were just happy to be away from the other piranha and not have to be looking over their shoulder all the time, kind of the fish version of the political life.

As our stay crept to an end, we came to marvel at the owner's success in eradicating every last tiny vestige of civilization and even began to appreciate the purity of his creation, a true and authentic fish camp. On our final evening, the camp chef, perhaps out of nostalgia for his days at the four-star hotel, took off early from his day job of herding cows through the swamp and prepared us a sumptuous stew of piranha heads, which we had caught ourselves. It was quite good, with just a tiny bite to it.

That night as I lay awake on my cast-iron cot I heard Hempthorn stir. "What are you doing?" I asked.

"I have to go to the bathroom," he said.

"Are you crazy?" I said. "It's pitch black. You can't see a thing."

"When you gotta go you gotta go," he said.

"Not me," I said. "I'm not going to the bathroom till we're back in civilization."

Hempthorn began moving gingerly toward the door. "Oh no, they're back!" he cried. "I can feel creepy-crawly things all around my feet! Flick on the flashlight for me, will you?"

"Sorry," I said. "The flashlight hasn't worked ever since I

hurled it at the five-pound bat the other night. But wait a sec. I'll strike a match and maybe that will solve the problem."

I struck a match and held it down toward the floor. "It's not going to work," I said. "I don't know what they made this hovel out of, but it won't catch fire."

"But did you see what's on the floor?"

"Yes, I did," I said. "And I've got some good news for you, Hempthorn, and some bad news. The good news is, tonight the creepy-crawly things aren't frogs. And you don't want to know the bad news."

Bearness

Was Goldilocks stupid or what? If so, she wasn't the only one. It seems to me there is an overabundance of people who don't have a proper appreciation of bears. I don't know how many tourists I've seen walk right up to a bear and offer it a snack. Sometimes this kind of tourist will stand out in a crowd of other tourists, simply because he fairly exudes a certain residue of self-confidence, and also because he's in a bunch of little pieces. On the other hand there are people who are terrified of bears, and think wild places would be a whole lot nicer if there were no bears at all there. Aldo Leopold once wrote something to the effect that a spruce tree with a grouse in it is totally different from a spruce tree without a grouse in it. I think Aldo would say pretty much the same thing about bears. A forest with a bear in it is totally different from a forest without a bear in it. It's something not quite definable. I'll call it "bearness."

When I was a boy, my friends and I did all of our first

camping trips in farm woodlots. The woodlots did not have any bears in them. This was not an oversight on our part. We did, of course, let on there was at least a possibility a bear or two could be occupying the woodlot.

"I haven't noticed any bear sign around here," Vern would say. Even if there had been bear sign, Vern wouldn't have recognized it as such anyway. He was merely inventing a little ambiance for the camping trip. Furthermore, if there had been bear sign in that particular woodlot, the bear would have had to mail it in. There were no bears anywhere close to where we lived, a situation with which, as ten-year-olds, we were generally quite pleased. But a camping trip without at least the potential of bears is not really a camping trip.

We were twelve years old or so when an actual bear first enlivened one of our outings. It was on our very first real camping trip into the mountains near our homes. (By "real" I mean our camp was far enough away that we couldn't run home when it got dark. Come what may, we were committed to the night.) Kenny had gotten up in the middle of the night to answer a call of nature. Twenty feet from him, just on the other side of tiny Schweitzer Creek, a huge old black bear plodded by as if going down to the corner store for a quart of milk. It paid no attention to Kenny. That was not true of Kenny, in regard to the bear. The only trouble the bear caused was that for several hours after he saw it, Kenny couldn't get his eyelids to stretch down over his eyeballs. So he was as good as awake all night, kind of like a sentry, which would have been reassuring to the rest of us if we had known.

At breakfast the next morning, Kenny casually mentioned that while he was out sprinkling the ground next to the tent a big old bear had practically strolled through camp. "I reckon that bear would go upward of three hundred pounds," he said, calmly munching a piece of bacon flambé. "I'd have woke you guys up, except it might have startled the heck out of you to see a bear that close and—"

The Bear in the Attic

"Hey!" Norm yelled at Kenny. "What's that wet streak going clear up the side of my tent? I hope that isn't . . . !"

Naturally, we didn't believe Kenny at first, but later we found the bear's tracks next to the creek. Suddenly our little outing was transformed into something wonderful. This was the real stuff! We were really camping now! We were really outdoorsmen at last! We were really not going to get a bit of sleep for the rest of the camping trip. This was so great!

For all the time I've spent wandering about in the woods, I've seldom run into bears at close range. Three times, though, I've had a bear saunter by me at night scarcely a stone's throw from my sleeping bag. Once was up in the Cascade Mountains of Washington; another time, in the Cabinet Mountains of Montana; and the third time, in the Selkirk Mountains of Idaho. All three of those bears looked remarkably alike. I know because I studied each of them with considerable interest. I sometimes wonder if they're not the same bear that strolled through our camp on Schweitzer Creek half a century ago, a ghost bear perhaps, a big old ghost bear following me around just to keep me tuned in to the bearness of the mountains. If that's its intent, it works.

Once Vern and I were nearly killed in grizzly country. We were both about sixteen and had been hiking for a week through the Cabinet Mountains, still total wilderness back then, with long stretches unmarred by so much as a trail. Early one morning we were working our way around the edge of a small mountain lake when we came across a grizzly track in some mud. The track was so fresh its edges were still crumbling in. How did we know it was a grizzly track when we had never before actually seen a grizzly track? Listen, you don't need a grizzly standing in it to know it's a grizzly track. It was a grizzly track. Now, I like bearness, and I like to have it in my woods and in my mountains, but that track was about as much bearness as I could stand at the moment. It was just too concentrated. The grizz was finger-lickin' close, but we didn't know exactly where—ahead of us, behind, above, below.

Then, scarcely three feet away, a patch of brush exploded with an angry roar. By the time we touched back down on the trail, we realized it was only a grouse—a killer grouse, though. Under the right circumstances, a grouse can be almost as lethal as a grizzly.

A sure-fire way to avoid seeing a bear is to go hunting for one. Or take me hunting for one. That's my experience anyway. You have a problem bear in your neck of the woods, I'll come hunt it. That critter will vanish like a puff of smoke a week before I get there and not appear again until a week after I'm back home. I've rid whole mountain ranges of entire populations of bears merely by driving through with a rifle in the car. Furthermore, I can keep them away merely by pretending to think about hunting them. Bears can sense that. I have friends who will testify to this. Not only won't they take me bear hunting with them, my so-called friends actually have the audacity to stop by the house and ask me not to think about bears while they're out bear hunting without me. All I can think of for the rest of the day, of course, is that my friends are out bear hunting without me. Serves them right, if you ask me. Come to think of it, maybe that's why bears never bother me out in the woods. They know I'm their friend, a protector, a kind of early-warning system for them. If bears ever take over the world, I hope they remember that.

When I was a boy, we had a ratty old bearskin coat knocking around the house for years. My grandmother told me my grandfather had given it to her on some distant wedding anniversary.

"Wow," I said. "I bet it was beautiful back then."

"Nope," Gram said. "It looked about the same then as it does now. That's one reason your grandpap ain't around no more."

Surely, she jested. In any case, I got a lot of mileage out of that old coat. For example, my mother would say, "I'm going to take a nap. Wake me at three sharp."

"You got it," I'd say.

At only eight years old, I was one of the best waker-uppers you can even imagine. I'd slip into that coat like Superman slipping into a phone booth, pull it up over my head, and, *ta-TAHH*, instantly be transformed into Superwakerupper. When I woke somebody, they stayed awoke. I'd go into Mom's bedroom and give her a hard shake, accompanied by appropriate sound effects. She wouldn't blink an eye for the next forty-eight hours. On occasion, some passersby might have thought they'd witnessed a crazed woman chasing a bear across a hayfield, but in truth it was only a mother who had requested a wake-up call.

I think bears get a kick out of scaring people. If he had known of it, I think the very first owner of that ratty old bearskin coat would have appreciated my effort to carry on a fine old tradition, a tradition that even today tells us deep down that Goldilocks must have been a really stupid little girl.

The Shooting Lesson

It was tragic. It was outrageous. Crazy Eddie Muldoon and I were both already nine years old that long hot summer and neither of us had yet shot a real gun. This was through no fault of our own. It seemed as if half the people in the county had nothing more on their minds than prohibiting Eddie and me from shooting real guns. The closer we got to our own homes the greater the interest in keeping real guns out of our hands. Inside our homes, preoccupation with keeping us gunless reached a fever pitch.

My father having died when I was six, I now lived with a family of women: my grandmother, my mother, and my sister, none of whom had the slightest interest in guns or hunting. We did keep an imaginary pistol in the house, though. Whenever there was a knock on the door late at night, my sister was supposed to shout out, "Do you want the gun, Ma, do you want the gun?" This proved highly effective in frightening off burglars, murderers, madmen, and neighbors stopping by to borrow a cup of sugar. Generally speaking, no one was ever there when we answered the door late at night. Mom was so pleased with the imaginary pistol that even if we'd had an actual gun in the house, she would probably have sold it. Ammunition for an imaginary pistol is so much cheaper.

Eddie's house, in contrast to my own, was crammed with real guns. Utterly delicious, drool-over rifles and shotguns decorated every wall of the living room and were topics of endless conversation among hunting men who stopped by for a visit. Eddie and I loved hearing the stories of those guns, which we itched to get into our own hands. We had been firmly informed, however, that it would be extremely dangerous for us to lay so much as a finger on a single rifle or shotgun. The danger came not so much from the gun as from Eddie's mother:

"Your howls will be echoing off the mountain for a week!"

Talk about your child abuse. But it worked. Eddie and I never touched a gun.

Every once in a while we would beg Eddie's father to teach us how to shoot. He would study us silently for a few moments. Then his face would twitch and he would go back to reading his newspaper. We knew that the day he'd teach us to shoot real guns lay far off in the distant future, probably when we were as old and cranky as he was.

We each did have a BB gun. Eddie and I had practically carpeted the yards of our homes with the tiny golden orbs. When we first got the BB guns, a rumor spread among the local population of swallows that a deadly threat had arrived. The rumor soon proved unfounded. If anything, the swallows regarded Eddie and me not as a threat but an amusement. They swooped and darted about us with impunity. We couldn't quite make out the tiny, infuriating grins on their faces, but we knew they were there.

As it turned out, Eddie's father missed the chance to give

us our first lesson at shooting a real gun. I'm sure it was a matter of deep regret for him, despite his success at concealing any disappointment. Our instructor, by sheer chance, happened to be a skinny old man we'd never seen or even heard of before, a complete stranger. That might possibly have explained his willingness to teach us to shoot.

Eddie and I were walking along the road one day when a battered old pickup truck pulled up next to us. The driver leaned out and shouted to us, "Mighty hot out to be hoofin' it. You boys hop right on in here."

Eddie and I had never before been offered a ride, so we were not about to turn one down, even though we were scarcely a hundred yards from the Muldoon house. We piled in beside the old man, not realizing at the time that he was crazy. Mr. Muldoon himself said so, once he learned the old man had given us our first shooting lesson.

"Pritchard's the name!" the old man shouted at us, grinding the pickup into gear and turning out in front of a logging truck. "I live up the road here a spell and—dang screeching! So what you boys up to today?"

"Just out hunting with our BB guns," Eddie answered. "Didn't get nothin' though."

"BB guns!" Mr. Pritchard snorted. "Why, when I was your age, I'd already shot a dozen deer, three or four elk, a moose or two, and a few hundred smaller critters! What's two strappin' younguns like you still foolin' with BB guns for?"

Well, naturally we were embarrassed. "My pa won't teach us how to shoot real guns," Eddie said. "He says BB guns are good enough for us."

Mr. Pritchard responded loudly to this injustice. "BB guns!" he ranted. "Why, my pap give me my first twenty-two when I was four years old. Had my own thirty-ought-six and a twelve-gauge shotgun by the time I was five! BB guns! I tell you what, boys! You come on up to my place sometime and I'll teach you how to shoot! I live on, ah, Goose Crick Road.

Just remember Goose Crick Road! You'll see my name on the mailbox! Pritchard! Shot my first deer up there on, ah, Goose Crick! I wasn't quite five years old yet, so naturally I was pretty short and . . . !"

By the time Mr. Pritchard finished telling us about his first deer we were three miles past Eddie's house. "We get off here, Mr. Pritchard," Eddie told him. "Thanks for the ride."

"And for offering to teach us how to shoot," I added. "We'll take you up on that."

"You bet!" shouted Mr. Pritchard. "Just remember, Goose Crick Road!"

Walking the three miles back to Eddie's house, I said, "That was awful nice of Mr. Pritchard, offering to teach us how to shoot real guns. But I've never heard of Goose Crick Road."

"Me neither," Eddie said. "But I figured he meant Goat Crick Road. He's pretty old and it's probably easy for him to get mixed up like that. We'll ride our bikes up there tomorrow."

Eddie had been right. Two hours of pedaling the next day brought us, coated with a muddy mixture of sweat and dust, to the mailbox on which was faintly lettered the name Pritchard. A house of sorts sat back off the road amid a clutter of outbuildings. In a rocking chair on the rickety porch sat a large, plump woman. She appeared to be airing her bare feet, while she fanned herself with a little fan she had probably made herself out of a sheet of tablet paper. She paused in midrock and stared out at us, as if she had never seen a couple of boys before.

"My goodness," she said as we wheeled our bikes up to the house. "You fellas look like you rid them bikes one far piece. What brings you up this way?"

"Mr. Pritchard," Eddie said. "Mr. Pritchard picked us up along the road yesterday and he promised to teach us how to shoot real guns."

"Mr. Pritchard? Real guns?" She shook her head, as if not quite able to come to grips with the thought. Then she roared out a command. "Harold! Harold, get your bony old carcass out here! You got company!"

"Company? Who?"

"Two little boys! You told them you would teach them how to shoot real guns."

"Good gosh a-mighty! Tell 'em I ain't home!"

"You got ten seconds, Harold! These boys didn't ride all the way out here for you not to be home. Get out here! Now! And bring your twenty-two and a box of shells!"

Harold presently appeared in the doorway holding a twenty-two rifle and a box of shells. "Heh heh, how you boys doin'?" he shouted, which seemed to be his standard mode of speaking. "I didn't expect you quite so soon! Hope you didn't have too much trouble findin' the place! Well, now, if one of you fellas will fetch us some tin cans from that pile of trash over there, we'll set up some targets."

"You do you own fetchin', Harold," Mrs. Pritchard ordered. "I'm gonna get these boys some nice cool drinks of well water."

Mr. Pritchard turned out to be a wonderful teacher. As often happens with shooting lessons, his enthusiasm increased proportionately to the success of his pupils. Pretty soon he was hopping up and down and applauding every time we drilled a can. I doubt we could have found anyone better to give us our first shooting lesson with real guns. Overcome by his own enthusiasm, the old man soon joined right in with us, taking turns to plink a can off a log. Mrs. Pritchard, too, got caught up in the excitement, proving herself to be just as fine a shot as her husband, if not more so. She'd probably had a twenty-two at age four herself, even though she didn't mention it.

After we had exhausted the supply of ammunition, Mr. Pritchard said, "Well, it's been nice havin' you boys. Y'all come back any time. Have a nice ride home and—!" That's when he was interrupted by another roar from Mrs. Pritchard.

As we pulled into the Muldoon driveway, I said, "It's real nice of you to drive us and our bikes back home, Mr. Pritchard, it being so hot and all."

"Yeah," Eddie said. "You're sweatin' like a pig."

"Yup," said Mr. Pritchard.

Eddie's folks didn't seem too upset when Eddie informed them that Mr. Pritchard had given us our first lesson in shooting a real gun. "Old Harold Pritchard taught you to shoot?" Mr. Muldoon said. "He's crazier than I thought. Well, better him than me." He went back to reading his newspaper.

Strangely, my mother wasn't all that bothered either when I told her that old Mr. Pritchard had taught me how to shoot a real gun. Of course I was thirty-five years old by then, so that may have made a difference.

Dumb Feet

My feet are getting dumber, no doubt about it. For the past year or so, they have spent far too much time shuffling about on city sidewalks, carpeted floors, and smooth lawns. Any major ascents they've made have been on elevators and escalators. Under such conditions feet become soft, smug, and complacent, and they soon lose any sense of self-reliance. They dumb down.

If you hunt and fish, you need smart feet. You need feet that can look out for themselves, and you, too. You can't constantly be worrying about what they're up to. You're out to bag fish or game, not to baby-sit a couple of spoiled feet.

Let's say you're rushing up the side of a mountain in hopes of getting a shot at an elk before it disappears over a ridge. You can't be telling your feet, "Watch out for that loose rock, Lefty! Sharp stick ahead, Righty! Hole! Deep hole!"

After all, your feet are a whole lot closer to the terrain than you are. They should be able to exercise some initiative and judgments of their own. Nobody wants a dumb bird dog that has to be told every move to make. The same goes for feet.

It makes me a little sad that my feet have started to dumb down. There was a time when I'd put the IQ of my feet up against just about anybody's. They could walk logs, ford streams, leap from rock to rock, follow a game trail, do all the usual stuff without any great supervision from me. But soft living has dumbed them down.

Feet can get dumb before you know it. I have a friend who's a great hunter and fisherman, but for a while he spent far too much time in New York City. He came out to hunt chukars with me one fall, after his feet had been penned up all year in wing tips. We had no more than started hunting than one of his feet, not knowing any better, stepped on a rock about the size and shape of a basketball. The rock was right at the top of a slope that slanted sharply down into a creek bottom far below. It started to roll. When the other foot noticed its partner up on the round rock, it started hopping along after it, trying to get up on the rock, too, so as not to be left behind, and finally did so.

As the rock picked up momentum, neither of those feet had the slightest idea of what to do, and my friend had to take charge of them. What he did was to make those feet move really fast so that he might stay upright on the rock and not fall off and break a whole lot of bones, which was the only other option.

From watching him, one might easily have supposed that he had spent a lifetime practicing the art of rock rolling, or maybe had even performed in a circus, but he admitted later that this was his first effort and that his success at it was not so much a product of talent as incentive. Mere incentive, however, wasn't enough. The crash was spectacular. He suffered several compound fractures of his body, injuries so serious in fact that he was scarcely able to hunt another ten days before going in for repairs. That, of course, is an extreme example of dumb feet, but it gives you some idea of the mischief of which they are capable.

Perhaps the best intelligence test for feet is skittering, a concept with which all stream fishermen are familiar. For the enlightenment of all others, however, here is how skittering works.

You are fishing a stream. You are wearing hip waders. You have glimpsed signs of serious fish rising on the far side of the stream, just a few feet beyond your casting range. You ease farther out into the current but still can't quite reach the rising fish. You ease out farther. At this point, the force of the current and the buoyancy of the water combine to cause your feet to slip and slide along on the slick boulders of the streambed. They are engaged in skittering. You cannot lift either foot without being swept away. Your cast is still short of the rising fish. At this point smart feet go into a controlled skitter. They skitter you out the necessary distance for you to drop your fly on top of the fish, one of which instantly sucks it in and begins doing aerial acrobatics. Your full attention is now locked on the fish and its antics, and your feet are left to their own devices. They now have to make rapid and complex calculations as to how much freeboard is left in your waders, the force of the current, the increasing buoyancy of the water, the distance to the rapids that will suck you into oblivion, your anxiety level, heart rate, blood pressure, the tension on your line, and the appropriate route of retreat. They make subtle adjustments to compensate for all of these factors and slowly begin skittering you back toward shallower water, where you can then net your fish. Skittering demands smart feet.

Although all stream fishermen are familiar with skittering, their spouses may not be, and perhaps it is best to keep them in ignorance of that subject. When I first explained the concept of skittering to my wife, she instantly went out and bought me an inflatable fishing vest. She said she had no faith in a person whose feet are smarter than he is. Spouses are an odd lot.

At the moment, I would not trust my feet to skitter properly. They are just too dumb. But they were not always so.

I started educating my feet as soon as I was old enough to run wild over the countryside around our little farm. In those days it seemed as if the whole earth were carpeted with rusty nails, and stepping on nails and running them into bare feet was a common occurrence among my associates. I could have built a small house with all the nails I ran into my feet, which at that early stage of my life were still dumb as the stones they stubbed their toes on.

A rusty nail bites into your foot with a sharp pain, which then fades into a dull, throbbing ache, followed by blood poisoning and possible death. My mother found this degree of torment suffered by her young son to be insufficient. As soon as she detected that I'd run a rusty nail into my foot, she would haul me into the house and add to the torture. She kept a bottle of concentrated liquid fire in the medicine cabinet. I do not recall all the details, but I suppose she first donned an asbestos suit and gloves and then, grasping the bottle with tongs, dosed the wound thoroughly. I would then be allowed to ricochet freely about the house and awaken any person who happened to be napping within three miles of our farm. A few such treatments taught my feet to detect a rusty nail at three hundred yards. Their education had begun.

Slivers were another important element in the education of my feet. When I was about eight, I ran a huge slab of a sliver into my left foot. From then on, my only mode of locomotion was the right-sided hop. The sliver festered away there for a week or more. My mother came at me repeatedly with a needle, tweezers, and her bottle of fire, but she was less fleet by then, and I could escape her grasp by means of speed hopping.

One Sunday we went to a loggers' picnic. Mom mentioned to one of the loggers that I had a huge sliver in my foot and that I refused to let her operate on it. The logger took out his jackknife, held a lighted match to the blade, and announced to the assembled picnickers, "I can take out that sliver in nothing flat."

Nothing flat wasn't quick enough. My first hop covered a couple of yards, small yards with low fences, but it was executed from a dead stop. Observing my flight, a kangaroo would have been embarrassed by its own feeble efforts. Eventually, some loutish offspring of the loggers ran me down and gleefully hauled me back to the operating table, which by then had been cleared of picnic residue. A crowd soon gathered around the table to observe the operation, there being little entertainment in people's lives back then. As I recall, the removal of the splinter was relatively painless, obviously a great disappointment to the audience. But then Mom appeared in her asbestos suit with the bottle of liquid fire. She took a couple of bows. The audience broke into applause.

By the time I was ten, my feet had a Ph.D. in rusty nails, slivers, assorted stickers, sharp stones, nettles, thistles, and the odd deposit of fresh cow manure. They could read terrain like a textbook. They had become smart feet—feet that would serve me well in a lifetime of hunting and fishing. I guess it's about time I get them out in the field for a refresher course. Skittering season is almost here.

Of fire and the Night

Night is closing in on the trail. You're twenty miles back in the mountains but not exactly sure which twenty miles. A peculiar silence settles over the trail. Something moves among the gathering shadows. Or are those shadows? They may not be shadows. Try to ignore the shadows.

It's been a long, hard day, and bit by bit you have been transformed into a single, vertical, barely ambulatory ache. All that awaits you now is another long, lonely night on the hard, cold ground. "What am I doing out here?" you ask yourself. "I must be mad!" Indeed, you are mad. All available evidence points toward your being stark raving mad. Otherwise right now you could be warm and cozy and stretched out in front of your beloved TV, munching popcorn and swigging down an ice-cold brew, just like a civilized person. "Oh well," you sigh to yourself. "I'd better stop and get a fire going."

An hour later you're happily poking at a blazing fire with a stick. Boy, those poor miserable devils stuck at home, you think. They don't know what they're missing.

Surely, we've all known that miracle of revival brought about by the dancing flames of a campfire. At least I have. One night in particular comes to mind. Not that I've ever been lost, mind you, but I do recall a time when my only points of reference were a rock and a hard place. The snow was a foot deep and deepening by the minute. I was bone tired and limping badly because of an injured knee. Furthermore, the logging road where I expected to meet up with my hunting partner had vanished—gone south—evaporated! Treacherous road. I would have cursed it roundly had my last bit of undrained energy been sufficient to do so. I had also begun to detect signs of hypothermia coming on—chills and drowsiness. Fortunately, I remained free of hallucinations, for otherwise I would have missed the family of Sasquatches frolicking among the shadows.

As darkness tightened its noose around me, I began to experience a peculiar feeling, a feeling perhaps similar to the one some of my friends refer to as "scared spitless." But I knew what I needed—a fire! No firewood was immediately apparent, but I did notice some promising bumps in the snow. I dug down through the bumps and found some slender logs, birch logs in fact. Not only did I now have my fuel, I had my fire starter: shredded birch bark. A fire the size of your father's Oldsmobile soon blazed merrily away, driving back the cold and the night. "Shucks," I said to myself. "I could stay out here all winter if I had to. Or at least until that next Sonics game." I leaned back against the rock, propped my feet on the hard place, and stuffed my pipe with English rough-cut, which I ignited with an ember from my fire. This truly was the life.

In the interest of public disclosure, I must disabuse the reader of any illusion that might have arisen out of the above account that I am an expert fire builder. I am not. To the contrary, I am famous among my friends for my total ineptitude in the art of creating a campfire. Yeah, yeah, I, too, read in the Boy Scout field manual all about whittling fuzz sticks and the like. All I ever got to burn was the fuzz! So I let my wife, Bun, build all our campfires, because it pleases her so much. "See, it's so easy," she says, giggling.

My lengthy experience at camping has taught me that, generally speaking, there are two basic kinds of campfires— the Smudge and the Inferno. The Smudge is the kind of fire you get when you are threatened with freezing to death. The Inferno is the kind of fire you cook over. The steak turns out medium rare and you turn out well done. When you hear a camp cook is smoking, it doesn't mean he's having a cigarette.

Despite my poor luck starting campfires, I am well aware that if I were to toss a soggy cigar butt out the window of my car during a torrential downpour, I would most likely burn down an entire national forest. I learned this when I was seven years old, even though I was not a serious cigar smoker at the time.

My good friend Crazy Eddie Muldoon showed up one day with a full box of wooden kitchen matches. Eddie informed me that if we wanted to escape second grade and become mountain men, it was high time we started practicing our technique for building campfires. It sounded good to me, as did all of Eddie's ideas.

We had discovered through experience over our meager years that in attempting to execute Eddie's ideas, if not ourselves, that it was best if we found some form of concealment from the ever-prying eyes of adults. A mountain-size pile of tree stumps towered up in the middle of one of the Muldoon pastures. It's quite possible that all the stumps ever cleared from the Muldoon farm had been heaped in that pile. The mountain of stumps provided both concealment and fuel. Eddie and I found a little private nook among the stumps and began experimenting with various methods of getting a tiny pile of sticks to catch fire. Occasionally, a sliver of flame would leap up briefly and then die out. Eddie worked his way through the entire box of matches without success. It was most discouraging. Upon later reflection, I am not at all sure that my mere presence didn't defeat Eddie's best efforts at getting a campfire started. As the last tiny wisp of smoke gave up the ghost, Eddie said, "Shoot! Well, anyway, I got this idea for a great deep-sea-diving outfit. You know how to swim?" A deep-sea-diving outfit! Sounded good to me.

As I lay in bed late that night, occasionally coughing up water, I happened to glance outside. It was bright as day out! I checked the clock. Midnight. And then I detected this peculiar roaring sound. I got up and went outside. The Muldoon mountain of stumps was shooting flames halfway to the moon! Waves of heat washed over me as I gazed in awe and a bit of terror from our front yard. That fire could have roasted wieners at a hundred yards.

Soon neighbors were racing in from miles away, expecting to see the Muldoon barn going up in flames. Instead, they found only a stump-pile fire—but one of spectacular and awesome proportions. Unbeknownst to the visitors, they were looking at the mother of all campfires! People wondered how on earth a stump pile could catch fire in the middle of the night. But they wondered only briefly. Suspicion almost instantly focused on Eddie and me.

"Pat and Eddie were playing with matches," was the report that soon made its way around the county. Eddie and I were deeply offended. Playing with matches, indeed! We had been conducting serious campfire research. And it was spectacularly successful. Later, someone asked Mr. Muldoon why he hadn't burned the stump pile himself. "I was afraid," he said.

Embers from the stump fire glowed for days afterward, as did Eddie's posterior, or at least so he reported to me. Even now, when dousing one of Bun's campfires, I envision once again in my mind's eye that towering inferno that seemingly had arisen from the dead remains of a box of matches and a few little sticks of wood.

"For heaven's sake, the fire is out!" Bun yells at me. "Enough with the water! You've flooded out the neighbors! You're eroding the campground!"

"Just a couple more bucketsful," I reply. "I think I just detected a wisp of steam, although it might have been some gnats passing through."

It's true, I may be a little overcautious with campfires, but I can tell you this: I'm never going to burn down a national forest, even in the off chance I do get a campfire started.

The Snow Cave

Our little adventure had started out innocently enough. My wife, Bun, and I were driving down through Idaho via a route that in December more than satisfies most travelers' appetite for adventure. But not for me. I'm a person who likes to get off the beaten path. Why else own a vehicle named Explorer? That's what you're supposed to do with such a vehicle—explore!

Taking a coffee break at a little roadside café, I said to Bun, "Boy, I've driven this highway so many times it's starting to get boring. Oh, sure, there are logging trucks, but other than those, where's the thrill? Hand me that map, Bun. Maybe I can find us a new route to Boise. I'm in the mood for exploration."

"No way," Bun said. "Now finish your coffee, Marco Polo, so we can get on the road. I want to be in Boise before the spring thaw."

"Very funny," I said, snatching the map from her. "We have plenty of time for a little adventure."

I don't mean to brag, but I am something of an expert when it comes to reading maps. "Ha! Look here, Bun," I said. "Here is a road that zooms straight as an arrow right out to the middle of Idaho and intersects with a highway to Boise. I didn't realize there was a road in all of Idaho this straight."

"Put on your glasses, Marco. That line you're tracing your finger along is a fold crease in the map."

"So it is. I was only checking to see if you were paying attention. You seemed a bit distracted. Ah, now here is the actual road I meant to show you. See, it wiggles through here and connects with the same highway to Boise."

"Hmm. I don't like the looks of those wiggles. They probably mean the road goes over some mountains. How do you know that road doesn't go over some terrible mountain pass?"

"Because I know there aren't any mountains in that part of Idaho, that's how. It's all flat country over there, pretty much. Anyway, where's your spirit of adventure?"

"I left it on a rock in the North Fork of the Clearwater River thirty years ago, along with the canoe, as you'll recall. You may also recall you predicted there were no rapids in that part of the river."

"That's what makes rapids so treacherous. They sneak in where they're not suppose to be. Surely you've heard the phrase 'treacherous rapids.' It's different with mountains. They stay put."

"Gee, I don't know. Your shortcuts are frightening enough in the summer. In winter? Well, I just hope you know what you're doing."

"Are you kidding? Look at this map. Did you ever see a safer-looking road? Take my word for it, this shortcut will be a piece of cake."

Four hours later, we were crawling up over a terrible mountain pass in a blizzard. So I was wrong. Mountains can be treacherous, too. Where these mountains had come from I had no idea. They must have been some renegades that broke off from the Sawtooth Range. Or maybe they had been thrown out of the range for being too wild and mean even for the Sawtooths. They were a nasty bunch, no doubt about that.

Gale-force winds buffeted the Explorer, which might easily have been blown off into one of the bottomless gorges except for the snowdrifts that lined the road on both sides. By no means entirely benevolent, the drifts had begun to cross the road both ahead of and behind us, like the closing teeth of some monstrous trap. Scarcely a minute passed that I wasn't confronted with a new threat.

"Surely you jest," I replied as we exploded through another drift.

"I most certainly do not!" Bun snapped. "That is, of course, if we manage to survive this shortcut of yours."

"Relax," I said. "If worse comes to worst and we actually do get snowbound up in this pass, remote as that possibility is, I will merely construct us a snow cave, in which we will be nice and comfy until—"

"Snow cave! Did I hear you say 'snow cave'?"

"Yes, indeed, a snow cave. Outdoorsmen who get trapped in storms routinely dig snow caves."

"If that's intended to reassure me, it's not working. I'll bet you've never constructed an actual snow cave in your entire life."

"I most certainly have."

"Oh, right! When was that, exactly?"

"Exactly? Well, when I was eight years old, to be exact."

"Eight years old!"

As I explained to Bun, it wasn't just my snow cave. Crazy Eddie Muldoon had helped me build it, so it was partly his. Eddie would no doubt claim it was *all* his, because he had come up with the idea in the first place.

A blizzard had blown into our county, making it much too dangerous for us country kids to go to school. As a result, Eddie and I were free to use the blizzard for sledding. There were few things we enjoyed more than a good blizzard. This one was exceptional in that it had formed a hard, icy crust on the surface of the snow so strong that even adults could stroll about on it without sinking, although most adults preferred to sit out the blizzard next to a roaring fire. As Eddie frequently observed, adults were boring.

Eddie had come up with the idea for us to equip our sleds with sails that, driven by the wind, sent us skimming across the polished crust of snow, over stumps, through fences, and into trees. It was fun. One day while we were resting and taking inventory of our injuries, Eddie said, "Wow! Look at that snowdrift. It's as big as a house!"

"Yeah," I said. "You know what, Eddie, I bet we could dig a tunnel into that drift and hollow out a cave."

"We could dig a tunnel into that drift and hollow us out a cave," Eddie said. "It'd be neat!"

"Great idea, Eddie."

"Yes, I'm glad I thought of it. I'll go get us some tools."

Eddie rushed off to the Muldoon barn and presently returned with a shovel and a rake with a broken handle. We used the shovel to carve out the tunnel and the rake to drag out the loose snow. After a couple of hours, we had a nice entry tunnel and a cave that was big enough for us even to stand up in. We preferred lying down.

"Whew!" Eddie said. "That was a lot of work. It's a nice cave though. Maybe you and me could spend the night here."

"Yeah!" I said. "We could bring some food and blankets from home. It'd be fun. But don't you think we should make the entry tunnel a little bigger."

"Naw. It's big enough for us to crawl through on our bellies. If it was any bigger it would let in too much cold, or maybe even mountain lions or wolves."

"We wouldn't want that," I said.

"No," Eddie said. "There are a lot of mountain lions and wolves out this time of year."

"I guess my mom probably wouldn't let me spend the night in the cave, much as I would like to."

"Mine neither."

About that time, as we learned later, Eddie's mother had begun to worry about our being out in the blizzard so long. She had no way of knowing, of course, that we were safe and comfortable in our snow cave. After the usual heated argument, she sent Mr. Muldoon grumbling and growling out into the blizzard to look for us.

Even as Mr. Muldoon searched the outbuildings for us, Eddie and I were thinking up ways to improve our cave. "Maybe we could build a little campfire in it," Eddie said. "We could poke a little chimney hole up through the snow crust."

"Your pa doesn't want us building any more campfires, Eddie. Remember last summer?"

"That was summer, Pat, when everything was dry. Pa wouldn't care if we built a little campfire in a snow cave."

"I suppose not. But maybe it would melt our cave."

"I don't think so. Eskimos must have fires in their igloos, and they don't melt."

While this conversation was taking place, Mr. Muldoon wandered farther out into the blizzard, still grumbling and growling, and occasionally bellowing out our names. Then, through the swirling haze of driven snow, he glimpsed our sleds, which we had stuck upright atop the huge drift. He walked across the hard crust toward the sleds. He was worried now. Maybe some wild creature had run us off. Wolves maybe. Good grief! Their den might even be close by.

Eddie leaned over and peered out our entrance tunnel. "Oh, no, it's starting to get dark!"

No words in the English language were more horrible to us than the phrase "get dark," except maybe the words Mr. Muldoon had used when he discovered our last campfire. Scarcely were the horrible words out of Eddie's mouth than we turned into a frenzy of activity, snatching up hats and

mittens, buckling galoshes, and grabbing rake and shovel. I for one was filled with an ominous foreboding that something dreadful was about to happen. Like it would turn pitch dark before I could get home!

"Wait!" Eddie whispered suddenly. "What's that?"

"I d-don't know. Something's w-walking on our roof!"

"Listen! I think I heard it gr-growl!"

"It's walking toward the sl-sleds, Eddie! It's right on top of us!"

Then it happened. An elongated shape shot down through the roof of our cave, accompanied by a hideous howl. Eddie screamed, "It's got us!" He struck out at the shape with the rake. The creature emitted another hideous roar. Eddie and I emitted hideous roars.

As the sequence of events was later reconstructed, Mr. Muldoon's immediate impression was that his leg had suddenly dropped into the den of a wild and vicious beast. The rake biting into his leg pretty much confirmed that impression. It was a fairly common mishap in those days to do a one-legger down a hole of some kind, leaving the other leg on the surface to race about in a circle while its owner expended his full supply of swear words. But Mr. Muldoon's reaction went way beyond the normal response to a one-legger, or so I judged, this being my only experience of viewing a one-legger from the bottom of the hole.

Eddie drew back the rake for another strike against the monster. It was at that moment I noticed the creature was wearing galoshes. How dangerous can a creature that wears galoshes be?

"Wait, Eddie, stop!" I shouted. "I think that's your pa's leg!"

"P-pa's l-leg?"

"Yeah. I think your pa just stuck his leg through our roof."

With much vigor but little success, Mr. Muldoon now appeared to be trying to retract his leg back to the surface.

"Well, shucks," Eddie said. "Pa's ruined our cave anyway.

We might as well grab hold of his leg and pull him the rest of the way down."

"Eddie," I said, "I don't think that's such a good—"

Before I could finish, Eddie had leaped up and locked his arms and legs around Mr. Muldoon's flailing extremity. This turned out to be just the incentive Mr. Muldoon needed, because both the leg and Eddie shot up and burst through the roof of the snow cave, sending crusts of snow flying in all directions. I rushed outside and peeked up over the edge of the drift. Mr. Muldoon and Eddie had both vanished. That was strange. They had been there but a second before. And then I saw Mr. Muldoon, a misty gray silhouette rapidly diminishing toward the distant porch light of the Muldoon house. I could just barely make out a small shapeless blob still clinging to his left leg. Mr. Muldoon recalled later that he had bounded off no more than twenty feet or so before he realized the shapeless blob on his leg was Eddie, but he said he had already shifted into his panic mode and felt he best let it run itself out before he bothered with Eddie. Anyway, he said, he figured if Eddie didn't shake off on the way in, it would be a simple matter to remove him once they got home. Mr. Muldoon always seemed to be sensible that way and take the long view of a situation.

Bun leaned forward to get a better look out the wind-shield. "I see lights. A snowplow! A snowplow! We're saved!"

"Too bad," I said. "I was rather counting on constructing another snow cave. Oh well, maybe next time."

The Unexplained

I am constantly bumping into The Unexplained, by which I mean those weird occurrences for which no apparent logical explanation exists. Here's an example.

One day while fishing a lake up in Canada, I pulled out my gold pocket watch only to have it spurt from my grasp and disappear over the side of the boat. The lake was at least three hundred feet deep at that point, so there was no hope of ever retrieving it. Now here's the weird thing. The following summer I was fishing this same lake but a good twenty miles from the spot where I had lost my watch. I was about to give up for the day and head back to camp when suddenly I hooked and eventually netted an eighteen-pound Kamloops trout.

That's it.

That's the weird thing. I caught an eighteen-pound fish!

My friends could scarcely believe it. Retch Sweeney said he couldn't have been more surprised if I'd caught a one-pound fish with my watch inside it. The only explanation for my catching the fish, as my friends pointed out, was—The Unexplained.

I once invited along on a canoe trip a young chap—Perkins, I'll call him—who knew absolutely nothing about the outdoors. Perkins was nice enough, but I found myself doing almost all the camp chores, because he was totally inept (or perhaps extremely clever) when it came to performing even the most routine bits of woodcraft. About halfway through the trip, a storm came up and stranded us on an island in the lake for nearly two days. As a result of the delay, we ran short of food before the end of the trip, without so much as a dry crust of bread between us for all of the last day. And we still had one more night of camping out before my wife would come to pick us up, provided she hadn't forgotten and gone off on a cruise. Starvation appeared imminent.

"Well, it looks like stone soup tonight," I said to Perkins. "See if you can find a nice tasty stone for us to boil."

"Fear not," said Perkins, who had a flare for the dramatic. "While you tie up and empty the canoes, set up camp, chop wood, build a fire, smooth out a spot for sleeping, and make us a shelter for the night, I will venture into yon forest and secure us some tasty nourishment."

"Try not to overdo," I said.

Two hours later Perkins returned. He was carrying a large iron skillet heaped high with spaghetti and meat sauce.

Without exchanging a word, we sat down on the ground and ate every speck of the spaghetti directly from the skillet. Afterward I scrubbed out the skillet with sand, and Perkins carried it back into the forest. Perhaps, I mused, the skillet is some kind of spaghetti trap, and he's resetting it for our breakfast. Sometime later Perkins returned, sans skillet but smelling slightly of bourbon, I thought.

"What did you think of our supper?" he asked.

"It was only lukewarm," I said. "Also, I prefer my spaghetti a bit more al dente. Nevertheless, it wasn't bad, particularly when I expected you to return with nothing more tasty than tree moss. I don't suppose you would care to tell me how you came across a skillet heaped with cooked spaghetti out in the middle of the wilderness."

"Woodcraft," Perkins replied.

Perkins would never reveal the true source of the spaghetti, so even now that mystery remains locked in the shadowy realm of—The Unexplained!

When I was only six years old, my grandmother taught me how to identify five different species of mushrooms. I would go out in the woods by myself and pick a bucketful and take them home to my mother. She would cook up the mushrooms for our supper, and they would be delicious. After supper we would relax in the living room and watch our shows, one of which I remember had this six-foot-tall yellow bird that danced and sang and looked something like my sister. When television came along, of course, we watched it instead. No, no, I am only jesting about the big yellow bird. The Unexplained, in this case, is why my folks would let a six-year-old kid, who didn't have that great of a reputation anyway, go out in the woods and pick wild mushrooms for the family to eat. Were they crazy or what?

There was one particular mushroom, Fungus X, that was a favorite of our family's, not only because it was delicious but because it could be found in great abundance in the mountains near our home. In college I happened to come across a mushroom identification book—now there was a novel idea—and I was shocked to learn that Mushroom X was listed as toxic. One of my professors was a well-known mycologist, not that he ever bothered me, but I'd heard that he was also an expert on mushrooms. So I stopped by his office one day and mentioned to him that I had just read in a mushroom book that Fungus X was toxic and here I had been eating it all my life.

The professor stared at me, obviously fascinated. "That explains so much," he said.

That was it. He never even thanked me for making a contribution to the science of mushrooms, whatever that contribution might have been—yet another example of The Unexplained.

One day when I was about twelve, I walked out of our house and noticed a large black bird—either a crow or a raven, I don't recall which—standing on the hood of our car. I walked toward it, expecting the bird to fly off. It didn't. It calmly sat there and watched me approach to within a couple of feet. And then it spoke. "Hello!" it said, clear as the proverbial bell. Perhaps the bird had never seen a person's jaw drop like an unhinged trapdoor before, because it emitted a loud squawk, leaped into the air, and flew off. I rushed back into the house to report this phenomenon to my folks and some of their friends with whom they were playing cards.

"A bird just spoke to me!" I shouted. "It was sitting on the hood of our car and actually spoke to me." This announcement clearly startled everyone, particularly the visitors. A thoughtful expression came over my mother's face. Her interest clearly growing in intensity over my amazing report, she said, "I was just trying to remember if we had mushrooms for dinner last night."

I don't care what anyone says or what vulgar interjections of disbelief may be shouted out, that bird did speak to me from the hood of our car, just before it leaped into the air and winged off into—The Unexplained.

Some friends of mine and I have a little competition every time we go out fishing to see who catches the biggest fish. When we get back together in the evening, each guy reports on the biggest fish he caught and released that day. Talk about your strange incidents, even though I'm considered the worst fisherman in the bunch, I've won every contest we've had this summer, yet again an example of—The Unexplained. Oh, sure, some of the guys have an explanation, but who pays any attention to sore losers?

Is there such a thing as luck? I think there is. Given any particular fishing trip, for example, one side of the boat will be luckier than the other. If I am out fishing with my friend Vern, for example, he somehow senses which side of the boat will be the luckiest that day and sits there. So naturally he catches more fish than I do. Sometimes the luckiest side is on the left, sometimes it is on the right, but Vern has this sixth sense for knowing which is the lucky one. I have given this phenomenon a great deal of thought over the years and have finally concluded it is yet another example of—The Unexplained.

Do such entities as water spirits exist? My grandson Daniel thinks they do. Once, I went out to my dock with the intention of taking my rubber boat upriver to do some fishing, only to discover the boat seriously deflated. This in itself was not a mystery—one of the valve caps that keep the air from leaking out of the boat had been removed. I mistakenly leaped to the conclusion that a little boy had removed the cap to see what was inside the boat. I further assumed that when he discovered it was only air, the little boy, whoever it might have been, had dropped the cap and gone off to find something more interesting. When I asked Daniel how he thought my rubber boat might have become deflated, he brought up the possibility of water spirits. They were something I had not considered before, but I now keep a sharp eye out for them, particularly when Daniel is around, because he seems to attract them. Of course, they could show up at any time, because you just never know when one of them might emerge from—The Unexplained.

Perhaps you, too, have noticed how a new gun will suddenly appear out of nowhere and show up in your gun case. It is a mystery that has plagued me for years. I suggested to my wife that it might be the gun fairy.

"The gun fairy?" she said. "That's a new one on me."

"Really?" I said. "You don't know about the gun fairy? Well, it is very much like the water spirits Daniel is so fond of. Both kinds of spirits are intent upon creating nothing but trouble for people. See, you were just innocently dusting the gun cabinet when you saw what you took to be a shotgun that you hadn't noticed before. So you counted the guns and sure enough there was an extra one there, although I should mention it is very bad luck to count guns. Anyone will tell you that. But what happens, you see, is in the middle of the night this little fairy sneaks another gun into a person's gun cabinet for the sole purpose of getting that person in trouble with his wife. Now I myself hadn't noticed that the gun fairy had been up to this mischief, but believe me I would have given it a stern warning if I'd caught it in the act and— What's that? Diamond necklace fairy? No, I don't believe I've heard of a diamond necklace fairy. But I'll tell you this—that's about the scariest fairy I've heard of yet! I just hope it doesn't show up around here anytime soon. Oh yeah, right, it would just be another example of—The Unexplained!

The Time Machine

Young Melvin Futz stopped by the other day and asked me to advance him five dollars on the yard work he does for me.

"Not a chance, Melvin," I told him. "You're already into me fifteen bucks. If I was going to invest in futures it wouldn't be in lawn mowings!"

"Hmmm," Melvin hmmmed. "Then maybe I could interest you in the time machine I built out in Pop's garage."

"You built a clock?"

"No, sir, the other kind of time machine. It beams you out into the future or back into the past. You pick a date, and for five bucks I beam you off to whenever you pick."

"How much to get back?"

"Fifty grand! Only kidding. All fares are round-trip."

I knew Melvin was a smart kid, so I thought maybe I shouldn't discourage his creativity by telling him I wasn't interested in seeing anything so stupid as his time machine.

We walked over to his dad's garage. Much to my surprise, the machine was quite impressive. I even recognized one of my old defunct computers protruding from a snarl of wires and assorted gizmos.

"Pretty nifty, Melvin," I said. "You probably could win some money if you entered your time machine in the fair—as a better mousetrap! Ha!" I couldn't help myself.

"Oh no, sir, it actually works. Well, sure, it had a few bugs in it at first."

"I bet."

"Yeah, I beamed Mr. Jurgans, the physics teacher, into the year 2020, and my video tracer showed he ended up simultaneously in both San Francisco and a suburb of Boston."

"He ended up in two different places simultaneously? That doesn't seem possible, Melvin."

"Oh, it's possible, all right. It just isn't pretty."

"I see. Have you beamed anyone else into the future?"

"Mr. Zumbo."

"Jim Zumbo, the hunting editor for *Outdoor Life*? To where did you beam him?"

"The year 3000. He wanted to see what the hunting would be like a millennium from now."

"Well, shucks, Melvin, why don't you beam me out there, too. It's always a blast, hunting with Zumbo."

"Okay, just have a seat on the swivel chair I've hooked up to the washing machine motor, while I set the timer for 3000. Oh, and I'll take my five dollars first. I've been having a little trouble with the return part of round-trips."

"Yeah, right. I bet you think I'm actually falling for your little joke. So, what's that switch you're about to throw, Mel . . . ?"

I opened my eyes. Well, I'd been asleep all along. Why I would dream of Melvin Futz and his ridiculous time machine I had no idea. Must be getting pretty short on dream ingredients, I thought. I blinked and looked around, but didn't recognize any of my surroundings. I seemed to be in a park in the middle of a small town. A frail old gentleman was sitting on a bench a few feet in front of me. I tapped him on the shoulder.

"Good gosh, man!" he yelped, leaping a good half inch in the air. "Don't do that! Scared the livin' . . . Say, where did you come from, anyway? I glanced back there no more than a couple seconds ago."

"Sorry, old-timer," I said. "Didn't mean to surprise you. Uh, this may sound a little odd, but can you tell me where I am?"

"Why sure, son. You're in the little town of Possum Flats."

"Possum *Flats*? But the town's on a hill."

"Yeah. What happened, years ago we used to have lots of road-killed possums hereabouts. Folks dried 'em and sold 'em as souvenirs, and kids even sailed 'em back and forth to each other through the air. Called 'em . . ."

"Right, possum flats. Say, I was wondering if you might have seen a friend of mine, Jim Zumbo, around here recently. He's a funny looking guy with a big mustache and a cowboy hat."

"Funny-looking? By cracky, I did see him. He come down out of park no more than an hour ago. Swearin' a blue streak, he was, with the name 'Melvin' poppin' up every so often. I think he headed into Hank's Barbershop down there on Main Street. Well, it's been nice talkin' to you, pardner, but I got to go take my boy fishin'."

"Your grandson, I suppose. It's nice you take him fishing."

"Oh, he ain't my grandson. He's the boy assigned to me. All us old fellas get boys assigned to us. Ten years old, Rufus is, a spunky kid with a mind like a sponge—a wet sponge! Har har har! But I'm workin' him up. Got to go now. See ya."

"One more thing, mister," I said. "Can you tell me the time?"

"Ten after nine."

"And the, uh, year?"

"You're startin' to spook me, stranger. The year is the same it's been all year—3000."

I headed down toward the barbershop, swearing a blue streak, with the name "Melvin" popping up every so often.

Zumbo was sitting in the barber's chair, getting his hair cut.

"Ye gawds! McManus!" he cried, obviously delighted to see me. "Can't I get away from you even when I flee into the thirtieth century?"

"No," I said. "What are you doing, Zum? You travel a thousand years through time and all you can think of is to get your hair cut?"

"It's only twenty-five cents! I couldn't turn it down."

"Twenty-five cents! Wow! That's really cheap." I studied Jim's haircut. "Then again, maybe not."

The barber said, "Your buddy here tells me he came in on the time machine. You must have, too."

"That's right!" I said. "Aren't you amazed?"

"Naw. Time travel's been around for a long while, ever since a kid by the name of Melvin Futz invented the first time machine back in the year 2000. It had some bugs in it, of course. One time he beamed a poor fellow into two different places at once. Well, it wasn't pretty. The fellow's head—"

"Stop!" I said. "I don't want to hear! Anyway, Jim, I understand you came out here to check on the hunting in the thirtieth century."

"I didn't intend to come at all, and if I ever get my hands on Melvin . . . Anyway, I figure since I'm here I might as well check on the hunting."

"Hunting is wonderful," said Hank. "So is fishing."

"Really," Jim said. "I thought hunting and fishing might be nothing more than footnotes in the history books by now."

"Well, they probably would have been, if we barbers hadn't taken over the world."

"You barbers run the world?" I said. "What happened to the lawyers?"

"We overthrew the lawyers when they weren't looking."

Hank went on to explain that just like almost everyone else, the lawyers had been living virtual lives on the Internet. And as if the lawyers hadn't made life complicated enough already, the Internet made it a whole lot more complicated. Finally, the Internet speeded up life to the point that folks were just barely hanging on. Eventually, about the one thing you couldn't buy or sell on the Internet was a haircut. So the only time people ever left their homes was to get their locks trimmed.

While they were off the Internet to get their hair cut, their barber would try to get them to talk about hunting and fishing and other interesting stuff, but they would say, "I don't have time to hunt and fish anymore. Wish I did but I don't."

"So we'd tell them," Hank explained, "you better vote for the Barber Party next election then. Our motto is, 'If you don't know where you're going, what's your hurry to get there?' And by golly if we didn't win the election by a landslide. Well, it turned out we were even better at running the country than we were at cutting hair."

"I should hope so," I said, studying Zumbo's shorn scalp. "So what changes did you make?"

"Well, the first thing we did was to kick out the lawyers. Then we shut down the Internet. You could practically hear the whole world heave a sigh of relief. That worked so well, we did away with computers entirely and even calculators. Before long, life had slowed down to a crawl. Of course, right away we knew that if people had a whole lot of time on their hands, they'd just sit in front of their televisions. So we did away with TV!"

"That sounds pretty darn drastic," I said.

"True, some folks were upset with us barbers for a while, but they got over it. Conversation in barbershops improved a thousandfold. People had started hunting and fishing and camping again and were out having these great adventures, and even if the adventure wasn't so great they could lie about it and make it seem great."

"Any criminal activity around here?" I asked. "Other than haircuts."

"Nope, we solved that problem early on. Figured we had to pay more attention to the way we brought up younguns. We looked around and saw we had a lot of old folks who, as you know, were practically useless. Well, we assigned each of them a child to hang out with. The youngsters threw a hissy fit, of course, but eventually they got to like hanging out with their very own old person. Because a geezer has nothing but time on his hands, he can spend some of it looking after his boy, teaching him to fish and camp or maybe how to whittle himself a slingshot. The kid gets to learn some interesting stuff and the geezer's got someone to practice his creative lying on."

"Sounds like a good trade-off," I said.

"Say, Hank," Zumbo said, fingering his scalp. "How come you don't have any mirrors in your barbershop? I've never seen a barbershop without mirrors before."

"Be thankful for small favors," I said. "What barber school did you go to anyway, Hank?"

"Didn't. Went to law school. So, anyway, you fellas are here to try out the hunting, is that right?"

"Right," Zumbo said. "What kind of game is available?"

"Just about anything you might want—deer, elk, antelope, buffalo, *Tyrannosaurus rex*, ducks, geese, pheasants, quail . . ."

"Jeepers criminey!" Zumbo exclaimed. "You mean you can actually hunt buffalo now?"

"Oh, sure," Hank said. "I haven't hunted them myself, but I understand their numbers are such that they blacken the prairie as far as the eye can see."

"Zumbo," I said, "did you miss something there?"

"And passenger pigeons," Hank added. "The flocks are so big they blot out the sun when they fly over."

"Passenger pigeons!" Zumbo said. "They've been extinct for twelve hundred years! Now I know you're joking."

"*Tyrannosaurus rex*, Jim!" I said. "You can hunt *Tyrannosaurus rex*!"

"Yeah, right," Jim said. "McManus, how many times do I have to tell you, don't believe everything you hear, particularly from barbers. Hank's pulling your leg."

"No, it's true," said Hank. "Don't you guys get it? Time machines have been perfected. Say you want to hunt buffalo or passenger pigeons. We beam you back to, say, the 1700s. You want to hunt *Tyrannosaurus rex*, we beam you back fifty million years or so."

"Sounds interesting," Zumbo said. "But maybe we better work our way up to *Tyrannosaurus rex*. How about a nice simple deer hunt in, oh, let's try the 1400s, just before Columbus arrived?"

"Done," Hank said. "I'll have your safari arranged by the time you get to the Big Beamer. Good luck!"

An hour later Zumbo and I were at the Big Beamer. Luke, our safari leader, asked what we were after. We told him whitetail deer.

"Good," Luke said. "My nerves aren't up to a *T-rex* hunt again anytime soon."

"Sounds scary," I said. "What kind of success rate do you have on *T-rex* hunts?"

"Sixty percent."

"That's fantastic!"

"I think so," Luke said. "I go out with ten hunters and come back with six. Well, let's go get those deer."

The time safari was a lot of fun but I didn't have any better luck hunting whitetail back in the fifteenth century than I do now. Zumbo, as usual, bagged a magnificent buck. I was surprised to see him boning out all the meat though.

"You're not planning on taking that meat back with us, are you?" I said. I'd had enough trouble shipping fish and game back from Alaska. I didn't see how Jim could expect to get venison shipped back over five hundred years.

"Well, I'm certainly not leaving it here to spoil," Zumbo said. "Either it goes or I eat it here."

"Hey, no problem," said Luke. "We'll beam your venison back, Jim, then beam Pat, and then you."

Moments later I popped into the Futz garage. Everything seemed exactly the same, as if I'd been gone but a second or two. Melvin still had his hand on the same switch as when he'd beamed me off into the thirtieth century.

"Boy, am I ever glad to be back," I said. "But, Melvin, I have to tell you, your time machine works absolutely great!"

"Thanks," he said, staring glumly at the pile of venison that had just been beamed in. "Too bad about Mr. Zumbo, though."

Tin Boat

As a writer, I have found it necessary over the years to correct certain mistakes of history. I don't mean that some historian made the mistake but that history itself made it. For example, I once wrote in a book that my 1951 high school football team had gone undefeated. Sometime later I was confronted by one of those individuals who insist on quibbling over every little detail.

"I just read in one of your books where you said your 1951 football team went undefeated," he said. "Well, I'll have you know my team beat your team in 1951!"

"So, what's your point?" I said.

Apparently struck speechless, the man wandered off, a dazed expression on his face. He obviously could not grasp the significance of what I had done. His football team had been far inferior to mine, having lost most of its games by the time we played each other. Its win over us was a fluke, a mistake of history, an error, a miscarriage of justice. I simply took a wrong and made it right.

History sometimes corrects its own mistakes. As I write this, the Christmas shopping season is crouched and about to spring, and it therefore seems appropriate at this time for me to report here upon one such recent correction by history its own self of an ancient wrong.

November 16, 1999. My wife, Bun, has just come in from the mailbox.

"Anything?" I ask.

"Not much. Oh, something you must have ordered from St. Nicholas International."

"I didn't order anything from St. Nicholas International. I've never even heard of such a company."

We now flash back in time to approximately the last ice age, which is to say the year I was six. In many ways, it was a good year, because my family and I did a lot of camping out that summer. In fact, we camped out quite a bit more than usual, mostly because our big old farmhouse had burned down. It was nice. We cooked over a campfire, dipped our water out of an icy spring, bathed in an icy creek, caught fish, picked berries and wild greens, and, for music, listened to the melodious songs of coyotes. Our nights were spent lying on the ground looking up at the stars."

"Wow, this is really neat," I said to my mother one night. "Do you suppose there are people just like us living up there somewhere among the stars?"

"Shut up," she replied.

You see, I was still under suspicion for arson. The theory was that I had set fire to the house playing with matches. Nothing was ever proved, however, not that that made any difference as far as my mother, father, and sister—an intolerant bunch if ever there was one—were concerned. In fact, I have never had any recollection whatsoever of *playing* with matches. Sure, I may have conducted a few scientific experiments, but that's about it. And even suppose a guy does make one little mistake, are you going to hold it against him forever?

Eventually my father found us an ancient but small log cabin some distance back in the mountains. As soon as a dead porcupine could be evicted, we moved in. Boy, I tell you, it is absolutely no fun at all to be scrunched into one little room with two surly adults and one teenage sister whose one immediate concern is to catch her little brother alone in a dark place. Dark place? No way that was going to happen.

The worst part of the months spent living in the cabin was the boredom. All my toys had burnt up in the fire, and I hadn't detected in my mother any sense of urgency to buy me some new ones.

"There's nothing to do!" I'd wail at my father.

"Here's a pencil," he'd say. "Go draw on the wall." Living in a decomposing log cabin isn't entirely without its perks.

Slowly my mother's feelings for me began to thaw out, and before long I thought nothing of approaching within five feet of her. As memory of her old house began to fade and her hopes and plans for the new house took shape, her mood improved considerably, and occasionally she would actually speak to me. Once, I remember she looked at me across the dinner table and right out of the blue said, "Eat your greens." That's when I knew everything was going to be all right.

And then one momentous day, Mom returned from town with a bag of groceries and another little sack. She handed me the sack. At first I thought it must be a trick, but no, the sack actually contained a toy! What kind of toy I didn't immediately know, because it was concealed in a little white box with black lettering on it that I couldn't read because I was illiterate. When I opened the box, my heart leaped up. Inside was a tiny tin boat! I shook the box and a cellophane bag containing some tiny round candles fell out. Candles? I pulled a set of instructions out of the box and studied the diagram.

Why, this was no ordinary boat you had to push around in the water. This was a steamboat! You placed a candle in the boat and somehow it heated the water and powered the boat! Ingenious!

I rushed out and hauled in our round galvanized metal bathtub. Then I began lugging up bucket after bucket of water from the creek to fill it. My father watched this process with mild interest, as he munched away on something my mother had brought from the store.

"What's going on?" he asked, casually popping a morsel into his mouth.

"Mom bought me a boat," I said. "A steamboat!"

I placed the little tin boat on the surface of the water.

"A steamboat?" Dad said, now getting interested. He squatted down for a better look. "How does it work?"

"Well, like this. You place one of these candles . . . one of these candles . . . they were right here a minute ago." I glanced at my father as he popped another morsel into his mouth and began to chew.

"NOOOOOOOOOO!"

"WHAT! WHAT!"

"You just ate my steamboat fuel! You ate all the little candles!"

"Candles? I thought they were candies! And pretty blah candies at that. No wonder I kept getting little strings caught in my teeth."

So there it was. I never got to see if the little tin steamboat actually worked, a source of regret for me and embarrassment for my father. (Mom: "You ate his *what*?") I can't recall Dad's saying the following but no doubt he did: "So, how did you plan to light the candles without any matches?"

The tin boat eventually vanished into the chaos of childhood, but I never forgot it. Indeed, half a century or so after my father ate its fuel, I wrote about the incident in a letter to one "Elf Watson, c/o Kris Kringle, North Pole." The letter was later published in one of my books.

Now back to November 1999. My wife hands me the little package. "Maybe it's a Christmas present," she says.

"Too small," I say. "I don't like Christmas presents this small."

Opening the package, I suddenly jerk back and gasp.

"What's wrong!" Bun yelps. "Is it your heart?"

"Sort of." I hold up the box for her to see.

"Oh my gosh!" Even though I am no longer illiterate, she reads aloud the black lettering on the side of the little white box: "Candle Powered Boats!"

A letter accompanies the boat.

> *Dear Pat,*
>
> *Recently, during a routine pre-archive audit, we discovered some correspondence between you and Elf Watson (Ret.), formerly of Hunting and Fishing Gifts. Elf Watson retired soon after your correspondence, citing job stress and other problems caused by being a supernatural being corresponding with a grown man. (This is hard on them.)*
>
> *What with one thing and another—we are very busy here, as I'm sure you can imagine!—your letter published by you as "Letter to Santa" in your book* Rubber Legs and White Tail-Hairs, *was never brought to my attention. An investigation soon revealed the fact that we had, in fact, misplaced your order for a tin steamboat all those years ago, Christmas of 1941. The world was in a big mess that year, as I'm sure you recall, and a few things slipped through the cracks. Please accept my apologies.*
>
> *Unfortunately, it is our policy not to pay interest or other recompense for such things—one or two wooden hoops misplaced for 150 years and we'd be out of business! Furthermore, it is our opinion that your letter has benefited you and many others, and you are in the end quite all right (well, that may be some exaggeration)*

*despite this inadvertent delay. However, it is our policy
that "The Customer Is Always Right," and in that spirit,
please find enclosed one tin steamboat with fuel.
Fondly,
Kris Kringle, Esq.(signed)
President and CEO
St. Nicholas International, Pty
Enclosure (1)
cc: Elf Watson (Ret.)*

The letter contained no clue as to the identity of the actual sender of the boat, unless, of course, it was, in fact . . . So anyway, let me just say this: Thanks, Kris!

The tin boat works wonderfully well, making a fine little putt-putt sound as it scurries around the bathtub. Its boiler somewhat blackened from candle smoke, it now rests among my other small treasures in a glassed-in bookcase in my office. "What's with the boat?" visitors ask.

"It's a long story," I explain, which usually sparks in them the sudden memory of a pressing engagement.

The little white box sits next to the boat, but the irony of the warning on its side eludes most visitors:

"Use only under adult supervision."

Yeah, right. Tell me about it.

What's in a Name

For years my fishing associates and I had gone by the casual but descriptive title of The Blight County Irregulars, meeting by chance at Kelly's Bar & Grill, where the topics of conversation would invariably turn to fishing and in particular to fly-fishing. Then one evening Bart Fleegle, the chiropractor, blurted out, "You know what? I think we should turn the Irregulars into an actual club."

"Good idea!" shouted Rosy McQuire, the beautician. "That might bring a little sense and order to this motley mob."

Everyone present agreed that a club was a good idea.

I quickly added my two cents' worth. "I don't like calling it a club. We need something with a little more class. How about calling it a society?"

"Yes, indeed," contributed Father Jimmy O'Brien, the Catholic priest. "I like that—The Blight County Fly-Fishing Society. We could have regular meetings, rules of order, collect dues, and even do good works, those sorts of things."

Several of the potential members questioned the need for good works. Bob Perkins, the car salesman, mentioned the possible threat of good works cutting into our fishing time.

"Good gosh, what was I thinking?" the priest responded. "I must have been carried away by the excitement of the moment."

Kelly walked out from behind the bar, wiping his hands on a towel. "Fly-Fishing Society!" he sneered. "You guys spend far more time shooting the bull than you do fly-fishing. You should call it The Blight County Bull Society—BS for short."

"Naw," I said. "That has too much of an agricultural ring to it. Besides, what we do is philosophize. Maybe we should call it The Blight County Fly-Fishing and Philosophical Society."

Shouts of approval went up from around the room, because there was general agreement among the Irregulars, myself included, that our discussions often attained the intellectual level of philosophical discourse. Here is just one actual example that I overheard this past weekend.

Voice One: "I was out fishing for Kokanee yesterday and caught quite a few, but danged if half the fish I hooked didn't get off."

Voice Two: "That's because their mouths are so soft the hooks pull loose. You'd think that if we can send a man to the moon we'd be able to come up with a better way to hook fish with soft mouths."

Voice Three: "I got an idea. How about a spring-loaded clamp? When the fish grabs the bait, the clamp snaps shut around its head!"

Voice One: "Might work. But you'd have to set the spring just right. Otherwise, you'd be seeing a lot of pictures of fishermen standing there holding up a string of fish heads!"

I don't mean to imply that all our conversations attain that high a level of intellectual brilliance. Such a thing is actually quite rare.

Fred Smithers, the high school vice principal, had a complaint. "I don't think we should name our society after the dumb county, or more specifically, the robber baron the county was named after. We should name it after a famous fisherman, someone like, say, Izaac Walton.

"Izaac's been taken already," I said. "But maybe we could name it after one of our own truly great Blight County fishermen. Any suggestions?"

The Irregulars to a man stared modestly down at the floor, each thinking he was the greatest fisherman ever to wet a fly in Blight County and mentally preparing his acceptance speech for the moment he received the nomination. When no nomination was forthcoming, the Irregulars took their eyes off the floor and shot one another irritable looks.

"Well," I said, "obviously no one here is going to get the nomination. So maybe we should select someone from the past. I happen to have a candidate in mind."

"You bet!" cried out Retch Sweeney, one step ahead of me. "Old Rancid Crabtree! We can call our club The Rancid Crabtree Fly-Fishing and Philosophical Society!"

Several of the more recent arrivals to Blight looked puzzled. "Who's this Rancid Crabtree?" Bart Fleegle asked.

The old-timers in the room all remembered Rancid Crabtree, of course. He had been the mentor to many of them in all things outdoors, and some things indoors, and they immediately shouted out their approval for naming our new organization The Rancid Crabtree Fly-Fishing and Philosophical Society. For the newcomers, I went on to explain about Crabtree.

He lived in a little shack back up against the mountain a few miles north of town. He never worked a single day in his entire life, as least as far as anyone knew or that Rancid himself would admit to.

"Sounds like a man I could learn from," said Dale Peas, the plumber.

"Indeed," I said. "We could all learn from Rancid. He was quite the philosopher, too, which makes him even more appropriate as an individual to be honored by our affixing his name to the society." I immediately recollected some of Rancid's favorite sayings:

"Ah ain't never been lost in the woods, no sir. But Ah been places where Ah had a mighty strong hankerin' to git to where Ah wasn't."

"Don't never take baths. Soap and water will eat holes in your protective crust and allow the jarms to git in."

"If a man ain't fishin' or huntin', he's fritterin' away his life, with maybe a couple exceptions."

"The two best times to go fishin' is when it's rainin' and when it ain't."

"Ah was born retired but Ah actually enjoy a bit of work from time to time, if it ain't too dull. Ah hear of a feller workin' at somethin' halfway entertainin', why Ah'll hop right up and go watch him do it."

After I had recited a few more of Rancid's favorite sayings, Father O'Brien glanced about the room. "Well, I can see that this Mr. Crabtree had a profound influence on the lads of Blight County. Do I assume correctly that he is no longer with us?"

"Only in spirit," I said. No sooner were those words out of my mouth than a strange sensation came over me, accompanied by a shudder. "Now that's eerie," I said. "I could almost sense Rancid's presence hovering here in this very room."

"Me, too," said Retch Sweeney. "Kind of lifted my neck hairs for a sec. But all it was, the breeze just shifted and put us downwind of the cattlemen's feed lot."

"So much for the poignant moment," I said.

Artie Arntson, the night manager at Blight City Supermarket ("We sell live bait"), then suggested that we have some patches made up to sew on our fishing vests to indicate that we are members of The Rancid Crabtree Fly-Fishing and Philosophical Society. Retch Sweeney, who is a pretty good artist, was assigned the task of designing the patch, with a likeness of the old woodsman in the center of it. Intent upon making his own creative contribution, Bart

Fleegle suggested that the words "Fly-Fishing" on the patch be spelled "Phly-Phishing."

Retch immediately objected. "We're going to spell it the right way or not at all," he told Bart. "I hate cutesy spelling."

I was a bit surprised to learn that Retch cared that much about spelling. It just goes to show that no matter how well you know a person, he can still surprise you.

Father O'Brien then stated that we should have some standards for admitting persons to the society. He said he thought only persons of high principle should be allowed in.

An uneasy silence fell upon the room, at last broken by Shorty Vetch. "I had a principle once," Shorty said, "but I've forgot what it was. It should still count, though."

Father O'Brien contemplated the problem of the forgotten principle. Finally, he allowed that it was far better to have had a principle once than never to have had one at all. Shorty most certainly would qualify for membership on that basis, he said, and the fact that Shorty supplied him with exceptionally effective dry flies had nothing to do with the decision. A collective sigh was heaved by the other Irregulars. If Shorty Vetch could be admitted to the Society, surely no one could be refused, convicted ax murderers being a possible exception.

A week later, when Retch Sweeney showed up at my house with the completed design of the patch, he responded crossly to my suggestion for a slight change. "Just like I told Fleegle, we ain't using any cutesy spelling on the patch, and I don't want to hear no more about it."

"You're probably right," I said. "Simple spelling is more appropriate, particularly considering our membership."

And that is how The Rancid Crabtree Fly-Fishing and Filosofical Society came into being.

Wrestling Toads

Speaking of wildlife, you're probably familiar with wrestling toads. No? Well, perhaps they're unique to Idaho. Come to think of it, I can't recall seeing wrestling toads in any other part of the country, although they are quite common here in Idaho, particularly in Blight County.

Toadus sumo, more commonly known as wrestling toads, are among the larger species of the toad family, or would be, if toads had families. Toads, for the most part, are loners, as are most individuals with large bulging eyes, grayish-brown warty skin, and the habit of snapping flies out of the air with their tongues. (This, I should point out, is in no way intended as a reference to my cousin Buford, particularly now that he's free on bail.)

Wrestling toads are most commonly spotted along road-sides, although occasionally they are encountered in the middle of a road, where they tend to resemble a Rorschach inkblot. Toads in general are at least five times smarter than frogs, but the concept of looking both ways before crossing a road still eludes them.

I have always been rather fond of toads, even to the extent that as a child I failed to recognize it as an insult when my older sister, Troll, would refer to me as "that little toad."

For many years we had a resident toad in our garden, and my mother came to regard it as something of a pet. When Mom was out picking peas or something, she would often talk to the toad, just as if it could understand her. "How are you this morning, Mr. Toad?" she'd say. "Well, that's nice to hear." As a little kid totally dependent on my mother, this made me extremely nervous.

Wrestling toads got their name because that is what they do, wrestle. One toad will be hopping along the edge of a road when it comes upon another toad approaching from the opposite direction. They each then rear up on their hind legs, inflate their bodies to about twice normal size, and begin to circle each other, their "arms," front legs actually, hanging akimbo. When one toad sees an opening in the other's defenses, he rushes in and tries to throw a half nelson around his opponent's neck, which would be much more effective if toads had necks. The half nelson having failed, the toads once again circle each other until suddenly one of them lunges in, thrusts an "arm" between the legs of the other toad, lifts him overhead, twirls a couple of times, and then throws his adversary in such a manner that he lands on his back, a position in which the losing toad is apparently assumed to be "pinned." The winning toad then performs a victory hop in the middle of the road, signaling that it is now ready to take on all comers, which in some cases happens to be a sixteen-wheeler.

Truck drivers, by the way, get a big kick out of giving a blast on the air horn whenever they see wrestling toads locked in combat. The startled toads leap about eight feet in the air, but without for an instant releasing their grasps on each other. This has given rise to speculation among truck drivers that the toads aren't actually wrestling.

We boys at Delmore Blight Grade School used to hold wrestling-toad competitions. My friend Crazy Eddie Muldoon had a champion wrestling toad, Bob, that he kept in a box and fed hundreds of dead flies to until even in its deflated state the toad looked as if it were about to explode, not a pretty sight even to imagine. One day at recess, a kid by the name of Jimmy Lee Jackson challenged Crazy Eddie to a wrestling-toad contest. Eddie just laughed, unable to believe anyone had a toad that could last five seconds with Bob. Then Jimmy Lee reached down and took the lid off a hatbox. He hauled out a toad that looked like a catcher's mitt with eyes. All the guys oohed and ahhed, except that is for Eddie, who figured Bob could make up in quickness what he lacked in size. Eddie agreed to the match.

The event was scheduled for morning recess the following day. Excitement flowed like static electricity through the male portion of the student body, and there was much betting of milk and lunch money on the outcome of the contest. The betting had to be kept secret from the teachers and, of course, the principal, Mr. Thornwood, because gambling was forbidden on school grounds, even though just going out for recess was pretty much of a gamble for the average kid at Delmore Blight.

The following morning, Eddie smuggled Bob into the classroom concealed in a paper sack and placed the sack under his desk, so that he could keep an eye on the toad until recess. What Eddie had forgotten was that Jimmy Lee's desk was right across the aisle from his. The two toads immediately sensed each other and inflated into fighting form. Eddie mopped sweat from his brow and prayed for recess, as he pretended to work a multiplication problem.

I should mention here that in those days teachers regarded chewing gum or eating candy in class as a capital offense, although actual execution of gum-chewers or candy-eaters was relatively rare. Nevertheless, Eddie almost suffered an infarction when our teacher, Mrs. Terwilliger, strolled down the aisle, tapping a ruler on the palm of her hand. She stopped at Eddie's desk.

"What's in the sack, Edward?" she asked in a tone that momentarily froze even Bob. Now, Eddie could easily have said the sack contained his grungy gym shorts and socks, but his mind had gone blank.

"Nothing," he said stupidly, when it was perfectly obvious something was in the sack.

"So, Edward, you think you can sneak candy right into the classroom without my noticing, do you?" Mrs. Terwilliger snarled. She snatched up the sack and thrust her hand into it.

You have to imagine poor Bob's emotional state at the time. Here he had been enclosed in a sack for almost an hour, tensed for combat all the while and expecting an adversary to come lunging in at him any moment. No one, of course, will ever know what went through the toad's mind when he looked up and saw Mrs. Terwilliger's hand suddenly thrust in at him.

The principal, Mr. Thornwood, was seated at his desk two floors above when the scream reached him with such force that his glasses flew off. Trembling at the thought of what horror must await him at the source of the scream, the principal rushed down the stairs and into the fourth-grade classroom.

The scene that greeted him comes to me now, as it probably did then, only in fragments. Fourth-graders were going this way and that. From time to time Mrs. Terwilliger bounded by, lashing her arm about as if cracking an invisible bullwhip. Clamped with all four legs in a classic toad hug around the teacher's wrist was the impetuous but hapless Bob. All the girls in class had now joined Mrs. Terwilliger in the audio portion of the proceedings. Some of them apparently had failed to recognize the creature as a mere toad; worse yet, others of them had recognized it as such. A few of the girls thought Bob was eating Mrs. Terwilliger and that they might be next on the menu. Their shrieks were deafening. Eddie, paralyzed from shock for several minutes, finally rushed in and snatched Bob off the teacher's wrist. An uneasy calm fell on the classroom. Mrs. Terwilliger was led away to the teacher's lounge. Mr. Thornwood went home with a tension headache. Eddie was later sentenced to thirty years in after-school detention, even though Mrs. Terwilliger held out for execution.

Riding home on the school bus that evening, Eddie removed his wrestling toad from the sack and set it on his knee. Bob, totally deflated, seemed even more bug-eyed than usual.

"Poor Bob," I said. "From the way Mrs. Terwilliger was whipping him around, I'm surprised he doesn't have whiplash."

Eddie lifted Bob up and inspected him. "I guess he's lucky he don't have a neck."

"I expect Bob has wrestled his last match, anyway," I said.

"Probably," Eddie said. "But what a match to go out a winner on, hunh, Bob?"

Bob did not reply.

Sling Bleed

Our small band of warriors waited and watched as far off over a distant plain a cloud of dust revealed the advance of the vast Persian army. A young archer next to me commented, "I hear the Persians number so many that when they fire their arrows they hide the sun."

"Good," I said, stealing a line from an ancient Greek. "Then we shall fight in the shade."

I dropped a stone into the cup of the sling and tried a practice shot. The stone *thwocked* hard against a far tree. I nodded with satisfaction. It was not the tree I had aimed at but at least it was a tree.

I had made the sling myself. The thongs consisted of rawhide boot laces. The perfect cup to hold the stone projectile had been discovered in a bedroom dresser drawer. It is not easy to find a perfect cup for a sling, but I had found one. I squinted my eyes in the direction of the advancing Persians.

"Let them come," I thought. "I and my sling with the perfect cup await them."

Suddenly, behind me, a peasant woman shrieked. I tried to ignore her but the shrieking got on my nerves. I turned and gave her a stern look. She was standing on a porch holding a fragment of a woman's undergarment. What do I, a warrior, know of such things? Gimme a break! I moved off to engage the Persian army, my retreat now cut off by the shrieking peasant woman.

Well, maybe there was not a Persian army advancing on my Idaho backyard. Testing a new version of an ancient weapon does tend to arouse fantasies, though.

I had completed the sling that very morning and, much to my surprise, found that with no great effort I could hurl a stone a good hundred yards with it. Well, fifty maybe. Which fifty was a different matter. Fortunately, I'd had the foresight to park my car in the garage before test-firing the sling, not that even there the car was entirely safe. Nevertheless, a dozen or so practice shots suggested that with enough effort I could become a pretty good slingman, although probably not of the caliber of the slingmen of the Roman legions, who could, I've read, hit an enemy warrior squarely between the eyes at one hundred yards. I figured that at one hundred yards I could give an enemy warrior a pretty good laugh.

This was by no means my first experience with a sling. When we were about nine years old, my friend Crazy Eddie Muldoon found plans for a sling in his *Boy's Book of Aggravations*, and he set to work immediately to construct one. His sling, too, was made of bootlaces, but the cup was formed from a rather prosaic piece of leather, the tongue Eddie had cut out of one of his father's old shoes. In Eddie's defense, there was no question the shoes were old, but as we learned too late, *all* of Mr. Muldoon's shoes were old. The shoe was by no means rendered useless, because, as Eddie pointed out to his father while being dragged out to the woodshed, all Mr.

Muldoon had to do was daub some black shoe polish on the top of his foot and no one could tell the difference.

It turned out that Eddie was a natural-born slingman, as he modestly pointed out to me. True, eight out of his first ten tries hit the target and, naturally, he could not help but brag endlessly about his marksmanship. I pointed out that of his two misses, one had broken a window in the Muldoon tool shed far off to his left, and the other had narrowly missed me, even though I was standing directly behind him.

"Besides that," I told him, "the broadside of a barn is a pretty big target."

Eddie shrugged. "It'll be a lot smaller target by next fall, when I take the sling to school for Show and Tell. It's perfect for Show and Tell."

"Well, maybe," I said. Eddie was right, though. The sling was perfect for Show and Tell. It was great! I couldn't believe I hadn't thought of it first. What rotten luck! A sling would be the most terrific thing anyone could bring in all year! Eddie would be the envy of the whole class! "It might be okay," I said.

Eddie grudgingly conceded that he might need a bit more practice. "Let's go see how it works with dirt clods."

Eddie and I were connoisseurs of dirt clods. A perfect dirt clod was just big enough to hold in the palm of your hand. It needed to be firm enough to throw but fragile enough to burst into a harmless cloud of dust upon encountering the head of the "enemy." A plowed field next to the county road provided us with an inexhaustible arsenal of dirt clods.

Eddie and I walked over to the field. "This will be fun," he said. "You run around out there, and I'll try to hit you with a dirt clod."

"Why don't you run around out there, and I try to hit you with a dirt clod?" I said.

"Because that's not the way it's done," Eddie explained.

"Okay," I said.

"Besides, it's my sling. But I'll let you have a turn. So start running."

I ran back and forth across the field while Eddie slung dirt clods. None of the clods came within twenty yards of me. The sun beat down ferociously on the plowed field, and I soon slowed to a walk. Eddie's shots didn't get any closer to me. Finally, I just stood still and looked at him. Clods sailed by far to my right and left. Some went almost straight up in the air and landed halfway between us. Eddie was becoming increasingly frustrated.

"You don't have to yawn!" he yelled at me. With a defeated shrug, he gave up and said I could have a turn with the sling.

Just as I reached for the sling, Eddie jerked it away. He smiled and motioned toward the road. Riding her bike up the road from the swimming hole on Sand Creek was none other than the powerful and evil Olga Bonemarrow, one of our classmates but also our sworn enemy. Bonemarrow was bigger than either of us, and twice as strong. Now, she wore only her bathing suit, and a ribbon with which she had tied back her wet hair. Even at that distance I could see the muscles rippling under bronze skin.

Eddie bent over and picked up the perfect dirt clod.

"Don't do it, Eddie," I warned. "It's too dangerous. Suppose you hit her. We'll never outrun her."

"Heh heh," Eddie replied. He fit the dirt clod snugly into the cup of the sling. "Remember, there's two of us and only one of her. She tries anything, we'll teach her a good lesson."

Bonemarrow pumped up the hill, concentrating on the road, looking neither left nor right.

I stepped back and crouched down, although no point within a fifty-yard radius of Eddie was actually safe. "Try not to hit her," I said. The sarcasm did not go unnoticed by Eddie. He gave me a sharp look, then took aim at Bonemarrow. Neither of us at the time was familiar with the phenomenon of the "miracle shot." So, of course, we had no expectation that we were about to witness one.

Eddie whipped the sling in a fast arc and sent the dirt clod hurtling in the general direction of the road, clearly one of his better shots, even though he had obviously given his target too much lead. The dirt clod rose higher and higher and then, miraculously, paused in flight, hovered up there in the empty air, *waiting* for Bonemarrow! Eddie and I watched in horror.

Then, like a guided missile not yet invented, that dirt clod curved downward, its homing instruments adjusting crosshairs until they found the target. Not until watching videos of "smart bombs" in the Gulf War have I seen any projectile perform like that hurtling dirt clod. It smacked the top of Olga's head dead center. *KerPLOOOF!*

Even as the cloud of dust drifted away it was apparent that Olga had already determined that dirt clods do not fall out of the sky on their own. By the time her vision cleared, she had already narrowed the possible culprits down to two. She stepped off her bike and laid it gently down in the ditch. Eddie and I calculated our lead on her. Not far enough. Not nearly far enough. Her white teeth gleaming brightly through the mask of dust, Olga vaulted the pole fence and streaked across the field. "Your turn," Eddie said, trying to hand me the sling.

Later, as we walked back to his house, Eddie daubed at his bloody nose. I was still trying to untwist my arm from between my shoulder blades. "At least we taught Olga a good lesson," I said.

"We did?"

"Yeah," I said. "We taught her she can beat up two of us just as easily as she can one."

Eddie nodded. "But the horrible part is, she took my sling."

"She did seem pretty happy about the sling. I don't know why, though. What's a girl want with a sling, anyway?"

"Let me explain it this way," Eddie said. "Show and Tell."

It made me shudder just to think about it.

A Big Chill

The sheer brilliance of the plan made me smile.

My assignment at school that day had been to give an oral report on a book I hadn't read. My fifth-grade teacher, Miss Ledbetter, had made it known to me that if I screwed up this report she would have all evidence of my existence erased from the entire universe. I would be a zero. Not only wouldn't I pass fifth grade, I wouldn't pass Go. I would proceed directly from Delmore Blight Grade School to a flophouse on skid row, where I would subsist by foraging in trash bins.

"Do you get the picture, Patrick?"

"Yes, ma'm," I mumbled, even as I searched frantically for an escape.

My plan originally started out as that old standard: Fake illness for the day, speed-read the stupid book, prepare the oral report, and the following day experience a miraculous recovery—"Maybe it was something I hate. I mean *ate.*"

My mom was no easy mark for a con job, though. Once, maybe twice before, I'd been able to pull off the too-sick-for-school scam. It was risky. Miss one little nuance in your performance and you were bat guano. Worse yet, you had to go to school anyway. ("Now, here's a question for the bat guano in the back of the room.") The school bullies left you alone for the day, though. ("Hey, man, I ain't touchin' that. Must have blown the too-sick-for-school ploy.")

I awoke early that morning and spent the first half hour getting in character—the Deathly Sick Person Gamely Fighting Off a Fatal Disease in Order to Drag Himself to School for Some Noble Cause.

Me: I've got to get to school no matter what, because the basketball team will lose without me for sure.

Mom: You're not on the basketball team.

Me: I'm not? I thought I was.

Mom: The fifth grade doesn't have a basketball team.

How do mothers know this stuff? I start to sweat. It looks like I'm trapped. (A faint but unpleasant odor of bat guano is detected.)

Mom: You're all sweaty and your face is all red. Maybe you actually are sick.

Me: Probably just a cold. My chest does feel a little funny though. (This is good. C'mon, Ma, think PNEUMONIA! PNEUMONIA! PNEUMONIA!)

Mom: Your chest? Well, maybe you'd better stay home today. You get yourself to bed and stay there, hear? I'm late for work. Gotta go."

Twenty minutes later I'd prepared myself a pot of hot chocolate and nine slices of cinnamon toast, fine-tuned the radio to a country/western station, and settled down to speed-read the assigned book, which I estimated would consume most of an hour. I glanced out the window. A single flake of snow drifted down. Could be the start of a blizzard that might get the school closed for the rest of the week. Do I really want to waste an hour on the book, when I might be saved by a blizzard? No, better not chance it.

At that moment I spotted a tall, gangly figure plodding through the snow toward the house. It was none other than my friend and mentor in all things wild and free, the odorous old woodsman, Rancid Crabtree. I beat him to the door.

"Hi, Rance! What's up?"

"Howdy, Patrick. Git yer ma fer me, will ya?"

"She's at work. It's Tuesday."

"Tuesday? Ah thought we jist had Tuesday."

"We did. Last week."

"Wahl, Ah'll be danged! Jist goes to show, time flies when a feller's havin' fun. Tuesday? How come you ain't in school then?"

"Sick. Pneumonia."

"Too bad. Anyways, Ah was headed out to Granite Lake to catch a mess of perch through the ice. Wondered if yer ma could use a batch. Ah ain't up to cleanin' and skinnin' more than a couple fer mawsef."

"I'm sure she'd love to get all the perch you want to give her, Rance. Shucks, I'll clean and skin them myself."

"In that case, Ah might as well let you clean and skin mine, too. Only need about a dozen. Too bad yer sick. Ah'd take you along and you could catch yer own perch. Wahl, Ah gotta get goin'. See ya later."

"Wait! Let's not be too hasty here, Rance."

Half an hour later we were at the lake.

Now here was the plan that made me smile. I go fishing with Rancid, catch a bunch of perch, get home before my mother, climb in bed and fake pneumonia for another day. Rancid drops off my perch later that evening and simply lets on that he had caught them. Perfect!

Rancid started to chop a hole in the ice but suddenly realized I needed the practice. Chopping a hole through a foot of ice with an ax was an art form I hadn't mastered.

"Gol-dang! If thet ain't about the worst ice-fishin' hole Ah ever seed! Looks like a giant funnel! Fella happen to step on the slope, he'd be funneled right down the hole!"

"Well, it's hard work," I complained. "Look, I got a blister."

"Ah wouldn't worry about it. Fast as you got cured of pneumonia, Ah figger thet blister will be gone in about a minute."

"That reminds me, Rance. You've got to remember, you didn't see me today."

"What? You expect me to lie?"

"Yes!"

"Okay. Jist wanted to be clear on it."

Two hours later we had more than enough perch for both of us.

"We'd better head in, Rance. That way I'll be home a couple hours before my mom gets off work. Now, here's the deal. You come by my house later this evening and drop off my perch, like they're a gift, see?"

"Right. And maw perch, too. Looks like Ah got a couple dozen Ah'll need cleaned and skinned."

As we packed up our fish and gear, Rancid turned philosophical. "Ah 'spect Ah never told you this, Patrick, but Ah almost done some work once."

"No, Rance, no! Tell me it's not true!"

"Sad to say, it's true all right. Warn't nothin' but greed on maw part. Before Ah come to maw senses, Ah'd actually picked up a shovel. But thet's when maw whole life flashed before maw eyes. Ah threw down thet shovel and Ah . . ."

Rancid reared back to demonstrate how he had thrown down that shovel in disgust at his own greed. And stepped onto the slope of the ice-fishing hole! He shot down into the hole in a perfect one-legger. As his other leg raced about in a circle on the surface of the ice, the old woodsman swore a multicolored streak, inserting my name into the stream of profanity every other word. Against my better judgment, I reached down and helped him extract himself from the hole. He was sopping wet.

"Gol-dang! We got to build a fahr before Ah freeze to death."

"No! No! We've got to drive home first!" I pleaded.

"Ain't n-no heater in the truck. Ah'd still f-freeze!"

"Maybe you'd freeze just a little bit," I said. But he wouldn't listen to reason.

We soon had a roaring fire going at the edge of the lake. "Now you look the t'other way," he warned me, "'cause Ah got to git outta maw wet clothes. Ah catch you lookin' maw way Ah'll whack you alongside the head."

"Don't worry."

Soon Rancid's clothes, right down to his faded red long johns, were suspended on branches over the fire. Steam poured off of them, as the old woodsman rotated next to the fire like a giant wiener on a stick. "Ahhhh! Ain't nothin' feels better than a roarin' fahr after a dunk in the lake. Ah'll count thet as maw bath fer this year! Ha! 'Nother five minutes maw clothes will be dry as toast."

A whiff of steam from the clothes momentarily blinded me. I feared for a few moments that it might melt my eyeballs but gradually my vision began to clear. Wiping away the tears, I thought I detected voices approaching.

"Patrick!"—a woman's voice, now up close. "My goodness, what are you doing out here?"

My vision snapped into focus. Mr. and Mrs. Withers, an old couple who lived down the road from us, were studying me intently. I shot a quick glance to the side. Rancid had vanished!

"Came out to catch a few perch," I said.

"What'd he say, Mother?" Mr. Withers shouted.

"He said he's fishing for perch!" Mrs. Withers shouted back.

"Oh. Well, I see he's picked up some old rags to burn. Mighty thoughtful of you, boy, cleaning up the litter. Looks like you got 'em dry enough to burn now, Patrick."

"Don't! They're not . . . !"

"You're welcome, Patrick. Always glad to lend a hand." He dumped Rancid's shirt into the fire.

Mrs. Withers gave a little jump and peered off into the woods. "My goodness, what was that mournful cry?"

"A bird, I think," I said. "Must have been a bird."

"Quite a nasty bird, if you ask me!" said Mrs. Withers.

"Well, just look at this," Mr. Withers said. "A rotten old pair of long johns! Wheee! Look at them blaze up!"

"There goes that bird again!" cried Mrs. Withers. "Either I'm hearing things or that is one very naughty bird!"

"Step aside, Patrick," Mr. Withers said, "while I knock these pants into the fire."

"Good heavens!" gasped Mrs. Withers. "There goes that nasty bird again. Something is sure setting it off."

"Well," Mr. Withers said, "we came out to get some perch ourselves and we better get started. Maybe we'll drop some perch off at your house this evening."

"No need!" I called after them. "No need! I got plenty!"

"Nice seeing you, too, Patrick," Mr. Withers shouted back.

Drat! The plan was unraveling!

Driving home in his old truck without the heater, Rancid growled at me, "You jist k-k-k-keep your eyes l-l-lookin' straight out front, iffen you knows what's good fer ya."

"I'm not looking at you, Rance. I almost blinded myself once today, I'm not about to risk my sight again. One thing, though, I wish you'd speed up. My mom will be heading home anytime now! Besides, my ears are frosting over."

"Ah ain't speedin' up when it's this cold! Hit a bump, somethin' important might break off."

As though anything on that old truck could be so important.

Later that evening, Rancid stopped by to drop off the perch. "Ah was jist wonderin' if Patrick managed to pull off his little ruse," he said. "Ah reckon he didn't, though. Otherwise, why would bat guano be answerin' the door."

In Judgment of Men

My father didn't hunt and therefore saw no need to own a gun. Nor did he feel he needed a gun for protection. A large, powerful man, he had for several years boxed in logging camp matches, where, he claimed, three-minute rounds and boxing gloves were reserved for sissies. The general lack of intruders in our area seemed a disappointment to him. Indeed, I think Dad relished the thought of encountering a hapless burglar prowling around the house. "I'd just like to see one break in here and try to steal something, assuming, of course, we had something to steal!" Taking into account the male tendency to invent heroic fictions of ourselves, I have no doubt that Dad felt confident he could deal bare-handed with any miscreant who might be dumb enough to venture into our abode. He would first scare the luckless fellow stiff and then chuck him like a javelin out into our hayfield.

My father died when I was still quite young, and a few years later my stepfather, Henri, or Hank as he was called, came on the scene. He wasn't a hunter either. I couldn't understand what my mother could possibly be thinking of, marrying yet another man who didn't hunt. Why she didn't consult me on the marriage, I'll never know, but if I'd had any say in the matter I certainly would have held out for a hunter. But no, Mom had to settle on Hank, a city person, who came with a complete set of totally useless sensibilities for life in the woods and on a farm. True, Hank had table manners and knew how to read and write and wasn't apt to commit any major indiscretions in polite company, and he could speak French, too, which certainly wasn't any great asset in Idaho. He also loved to cook and all too frequently turned out some incredibly hideous French cuisine from animal parts I won't even mention here, for fear of upsetting my stomach at even this late date. Hank liked to boast that the French used every part of a pig but the squeal. Well, I supplied the squeal every time Hank cooked.

My mother, of course, thought she had made a wonderful catch, but as far as I was concerned, Hank was worse than useless. He was a major liability. And worst of all, he didn't hunt! I simply could not forgive my mother for marrying him. After all, it wasn't as if there hadn't been plenty of old bachelors around who hunted. It wouldn't even have taken a whole lot of work to clean one of them up and make a decent husband out of him. Women can be so picky. Just because a man eats with a hunting knife—an art in itself, especially when it comes to peas—women will ignore all his other qualities and exclude him on that count alone. Go figure.

Begging being the chief currency of a child, I spent practically my life savings acquiring a BB gun. Stupidly, as I realized later, I should have gone straight for a .22 rifle—it would not have cost me more. Most of my friends the same age as I already had .22s. It was embarrassing. Sometimes we would go out to the gravel pit and take turns shooting at targets. A round of turns would sound like this: *POW! POW! POW! phimp! POW!* I'd complain to my mother that night at dinner.

"Shut up and eat your Ris de Veau et Cervelles au Beurre Noir." I'd translate that but, believe me, you don't want to know.

Far more enduring than the embarrassment, the years of shooting that BB gun eventually came very close to permanently marring my classic Irish profile. Because I had no one to instruct me properly on how to shoot a gun, I devised my own technique. Even though I'm right-handed, I shot the gun left-handed. But I used my right eye to sight with. This required that my nose be extended over and against the stock. It worked fine. In fact, I think my nose helped steady my aim. In all the times I fired the BB gun, I never once noticed even the slightest discomfort. But that is how improper technique often allows serious injury to creep up on you.

As time passed, I became accustomed to having Hank around. Despite his general uselessness, he was nice enough, and the only real cruelty he perpetrated against me was his French cooking. Mostly he was just a nuisance. He didn't fish and he didn't hunt and he regarded camping out as a form of insanity. Really, who needed him?

On my twelfth birthday, my mother bought me a .22 rifle, and about time, too. Still, I was by no means sure that the oblong package I was about to open wasn't a clever ruse consisting of school clothes weighted down with a few rocks. She had pulled this one on me before, disguising a package of pajamas in such as way that one easily might guess it contained an electric train. But finally there it was, a real .22 rifle. My heart leaped up.

"Now don't shoot anything," Mom advised.

"Oh," Hank said, standing there uselessly, observing. "A real gun. Very nice. I wish I had thought to get you something. Wait! I just remembered a little item I inherited from my father many years ago."

He jumped up and rushed off to his cluttered little den and returned a short while later with what appeared to be a soft leather case divided into several sections. Well, it was very nice and obviously expensive, but I had no use for such a case. That was Hank all over, nice but useless. He handed me the case. It was much heavier than I expected. I opened the three sections one by one. Each contained a piece of a 12-gauge side-by-side shotgun! The barrels were intricately engraved with fancy scrolls tinted a light tan color, with hunting scenes etched on the receiver. The gleaming stock swirled with the grains of some rare and exotic wood. Never in my life had I seen anything quite so beautiful.

Hank said he didn't know if the gun was worth anything and he hoped it wasn't worn out. His father had been a great hunter in his younger days, he said, and had brought the gun with him when he emigrated from France. He said even though it was old he hoped it would serve well enough, at least as a boy's first shotgun.

This only went to prove what good judgment of men I'd always known my mother to possess. I probably inherited the talent from her. From then on, my stepfather and I got along just fine. To Hank's delight, I and my shotgun brought him in a steady supply of wild game over the years—grouse, quail, pheasants, ducks, and rabbits—and he repaid me by dressing it all up in various kinds of sauces and rouxs and stews and generally making it quite inedible. But, hey, nobody's perfect.

That wonderful shotgun is long gone. When I went off to college, I left the gun with a neighbor friend to use in my absence. A few months later, the neighbor's house caught fire and burned to the ground. The news brought tears to my eyes. "Don't feel bad," the neighbor consoled me. "It waren't that much of a house anyways."

"House?" I said. *"House!"*

Although the shotgun is now but a bit of fading memory, it did leave a lasting impression on me. The first time I fired it I learned an important lesson, namely that it was not a good idea to use the same method of firing a 12-gauge shotgun that I had employed shooting my BB gun, the nose-on-the-stock technique. Right away it became apparent that my nose had been broken, but that was the least of my problems. I had just recently realized that girls were not of a different species and, weird as this may sound, I had suddenly been infused with a strange but frightening attraction to them. The trick now was to find a cute girl who might like dating a hunter, and one who also didn't mind going out in public with a boy whose nose protruded from the middle of his forehead.

Pest Power

Years ago I saw a movie in which a detective was showing a beautiful young woman visitor around a ranch somewhere in the South. At one point she cried out, "Oh, something is crawling on me!"

"Fire ants!" yelled the detective. He then tore off the beautiful young woman's clothes, brushed the ants off of her, scooped her up in his arms, and rushed her to the hospital. (Because of my keen interest in insects, I must mention here that I examined the beautiful young woman very closely to see if I could detect one of the ants. I saw not a single one.)

"Wow," I thought. "Those fire ants must really be vicious. I hope I never get attacked by them." I wasn't too worried, however, because fire ants live in the South and I live in the North.

Years later I found myself on a dove hunt in Alabama, which surprised me a good deal, as most things do. The guide took me out to the middle of a cornfield and posted me in a spot well out of range of the other hunters. As I was expressing my gratitude for his concern about my safety, I suddenly felt something crawling up one of my legs.

"Something's crawling up my leg," I said to the guide.

He glanced down at my feet. "Fahr ants," he drawled, biting off a chaw of tobacco. "You standin' on a hill of 'em."

Fire ants! The scene from the movie flashed sharp and full-blown into my consciousness. I panicked, even though the guide hadn't made a move toward me. Indeed, he seemed only casually interested in my plight.

"What shall I do?" I shouted at him.

"It's up to you," he drawled. "'Twas me, Ah think Ah'd git offen that anthill."

I sprang from the anthill, sealed off the upper part of my pant leg, and dispatched the intruders, relieved that I had got them before they got me. When I checked my leg, however, I discovered they had got me. Strangely, the bites were mildly annoying at worst and certainly a long way from fiery.

That's peculiar, I thought. If this is all there is to the bite of fire ants, why would the detective tear off all the beautiful young woman's clothes, brush the ants off of her, scoop her up in his arms, and rush her to the hospital? It didn't make any sense.

Or, I speculated to myself, it could be that I am immune to the bite of fire ants. After all, I'd long known that I have some kind of strange, perhaps even psychic, power over insects.

For example, it is not unusual that a fly will take a liking to me. Yes, a fly—the common housefly! A fly, for example, will have a thousand other places to go and things to do, like infecting people with deadly diseases, but instead it will insist upon walking across the page of a book I'm reading, obviously in an attempt to call attention to itself. I'll shoo it away, but a minute later it's back, strolling about the page. I cannot help but ponder the fly's odd behavior. What does it want from me? Is it trying to communicate something? Perhaps trapped within the fly is some deep emotion longing to be expressed, some great idea demanding to be articulated, some innate talent crying out to be freed—say, for instance, tap dancing. Tap dancing? My book slaps shut on the fly. Deadly disease is one thing, tap dancing is another.

And then there's this relationship I have with bees. A lot of bees hang out around our cabin in Idaho, but I don't bother them and they don't bother me. I think the bees regard me as harmless, as does almost everything. For years they have watched me come and go, puttering with this and that around their abodes. Not once have I been stung, even when I actively but unknowingly molest them.

Last summer I was digging a hole in the ground for a reason that escapes me at the moment. One of my teenage grandsons, attired only in shorts, stood off at a distance watching, not wishing to get too close to work. Suddenly, the boy bounded up in the air and yelled, "Ow!" He turned and started to run toward the cabin. At intervals along the way he yelled out "Ow!," accompanying each "ow" with a little leap, his legs churning wildly, as if he were climbing an invisible ladder. Watching these antics, I thought, We'd better have that kid looked at. He's not right. I went back to digging. It was then I discovered I was excavating a nest of yellow jackets.

The question is, What kind of thought process caused the yellow jackets to bypass me, the obvious culprit in the affair, and go straight for my innocent grandson, who was far removed from the action? I think it could only be something like this: "Pat's destroying our house! He couldn't have thought of this on his own! The kid must have put him up to it. Get the kid! Get the kid!"

A similar incident occurred later that summer. Just as darkness fell one evening, I was attempting to shove my canoe up onto its rack in a lean-to at the cabin. At that moment, my friend Dave, a tall, gangly fellow, stopped by and offered to help. He, too, was dressed only in shorts. I told him, "No thanks, I can get it. I just need to give the canoe one more hard push. There. Got it."

I turned around and was surprised to see Dave energetically performing a dance that I at first mistook for the Charleston, his long bare legs going this way and that, his long bare arms crisscrossing back and forth in front of them. Then he began to gyrate with such fury his glasses flew off. I started clapping rhythmically and shouting, "Go, Dave, go!" And he went. The last I saw of him, he was streaking down the road toward his home a few hundred yards distant, occasionally stopping to break into the Charleston or some other weird dance.

I shrugged and walked into the cabin, but a thought kept nagging at me. There was something slightly unusual about Dave's behavior. What was it? But of course! He forgot he had driven over in his car! Ha! And he thinks I'm absentminded.

The next day I went over to Dave's place to return his glasses and car. I mentioned that I had really enjoyed his little dance the night before.

"It wasn't a dance, you idiot!" he explained. "You smashed a bees' nest with your canoe!"

So there you have a repeat of the same phenomenon that had occurred earlier. The bees bypassed me, the obvious culprit, and took out their wrath on an innocent bystander.

"Don't you think this is amazing?" I said to my wife. "I must have some mysterious power over insects."

"Possibly," she replied. "Or it could be you need to shower more often."

But what do wives know about psychic powers, anyway?

A Fish for Vile

Every summer my cousin Vile would come to visit us on our Idaho farm for a month. My mother claimed his visit lasted only a couple of weeks, but she couldn't fool me. I knew Vile stayed for a whole month, maybe two, sucking all the joy out of my summer vacation.

Vile lived with his folks, my aunt Edna and uncle Leo, in a big city Back East, "Back East" being a geographical term applied to that portion of the United States lying east of Butte, Montana. It was his folks, Aunt Edna and Uncle Leo, who insisted that Vile visit us each summer. Vile hated his visits as much as I did, maybe even more, although that possibility is extremely remote.

I suspected that each summer Vile would throw a big fit and refuse to come. Otherwise, why did Aunt Edna and Uncle Leo ship him out in a crate? Only kidding. He came on the train. Still, it was easy to imagine him with his arms and legs splayed against the door frame of the train, while his parents, working in tandem, tried to pry loose his hands and feet in order to thrust him aboard.

The summer I was ten, I mentioned to my friend Crazy Eddie Muldoon that Vile was on his way to our farm.

"Great!" Eddie said. "We still have time to build a bent-tree snare. Or maybe a pit trap."

"Naw," I said. "Mom said we couldn't be mean to him."

"How come?"

"Beats me."

"Shucks," Eddie said. "No point in me hanging around then. See you after Vile leaves."

As Eddie walked off toward home, I fired a dirt clod at him. The clod exploded beautifully around his head and dropped him to his knees.

"No fair!" he yelled, shaking the dust out of his ears. "We had a truce!"

"The rules of war don't apply to deserters!" I yelled back. "I win!"

Vile arrived the next day.

"Hi, Vile," I greeted him, smiling, being nice.

"It's not 'Vile,' you idiot! It's Lyle!"

"Right," I said. "So, how was your train ride, Vile?"

Try as hard as you can, some people just won't respond to your being nice to them.

It wasn't as if Vile and I had nothing in common. We were both carbon-based life-forms. That's about it. Our differences were more numerous. He was rich; I was poor. He got straight A's in school; I didn't. He lived in a big city; I lived on a small farm.

"Ow!" I yelped. Cruel mothers in those days often caught your attention by thwacking your head with a thimble.

"Listen to me, young man, and no back talk!" Mom pleaded. "You get out there and entertain Lyle. And don't you dare be mean to him!" The thimble was poised to strike again.

"Okay, okay."

I walked into the living room. Vile was sitting on the sofa, reading the business section of the newspaper. The kid was disgusting!

"I just thought of something fun we can do, Vile."

"I doubt that."

"That it'll be fun?"

"No, that you thought! Ha!"

"Hey, Vile, just because I'm not supposed to hit you doesn't mean I won't. Now, listen to me. We can play war. Come on outside and I'll show you how."

"War? That does sound kind of interesting. But how will we know if one of us wins?"

"Don't worry, you'll know."

"No war!" Mom bellowed from the kitchen. "Here's an idea, Patrick. Why don't you take Vile fishing? *Lyle*, I mean, *Lyle!*"

"But, Ma—" A thimble flashed. "Good idea!"

An hour later I was headed down to the creek with a couple of fishing poles and a can of worms. Vile trudged along behind. At least I wouldn't be wasting good fishing on him— the fishing had been terrible for weeks. Occasionally, I'd haul in an eight-incher, but mostly they were small.

I baited up each of the fish poles, which were in fact poles, not rods. The poles were slender cedar saplings about ten feet long, with the same length of line and leader tied at the tip. The leader wasn't flimsy, either. In a pinch, you could have towed a truck out of a mud hole with it. The baiting completed, I heaved the lines over the top of the brush and plunked the sinkers and bait into the creek. Then I leaned the poles against the brush.

"When do we start fishing?" Vile said.

"We are fishing," I said. "This is how it's done. Every so often we grab a pole and jerk the line to see if we've caught a fish."

"I thought there was more to fishing."

"Nope. This is it. What do you think, fishing is some kind of sport or something?"

We lay back on the grass and waited. And waited. The sun slowly blazed its way across the sky. Vile said maybe next year he'd just join the French Foreign Legion before his folks could send him out to the farm.

"Good thinking," I said.

Suddenly the pole I'd assigned to Vile whipped down hard.

"I caught a fish!" he yelled, lunging for the butt of the pole, which was about to depart over the top of the brush.

"Quick, heave it back over your head!" I yelled, because it was obvious Vile had no understanding of proper fishing technique. Having never hooked a fish of this power myself, I thought maybe Vile had snagged a beaver swimming by. But no, with a hideous grunt, Vile twisted around, put his shoulder against the pole and with all his twinky strength heaved a monstrous fish up and over the brush. It plopped on the ground right next to me.

"I caught one! I caught a fish!" Vile squealed.

"A huge one, too," I said. I planted my foot on the fish and removed the hook.

"Ha! I caught a trout and you didn't," Vile said. "Some fisherman you are!"

"A trout? You think this is a trout, Vile? Hmmmm. Well, you're right about that."

"My first trout! Yea! Boy, they sure have funny lips don't they?"

"Yep. Your basic trout lips."

"You know what. I bet Aunt Brigitte will cook it for my supper."

"You never can tell," I said.

I cleaned the fish, hung it on a forked stick, and handed it to Vile. Then he rushed off to show his great 'trout' to Mom. As much as I would have liked to witness that scene, it occurred to me that the better part of valor might be to skip that particular spectacle. Surely, Vile's rage and disappointment upon learning the true species of his fish would linger on long enough for me to savor for some days afterward.

Also, a little delay in my arrival home would give Mom a little more time to see the humor in the situation. I strolled in about suppertime.

Mom stood at the stove. Vile hovered next to her, giving directions. "I think this side of my trout needs a little more browning."

"Whatever you say, Lyle," Mom replied. "After all, it's your trout."

Mom turned and smiled at me. It was one of those icy smiles, in which I detected more than a hint of malice. "Guess what, Patrick. Lyle was so excited about catching his first 'trout' that I couldn't disappoint him by not cooking it for his supper. But after all, it was you who took him fishing. So I made him promise to share his 'trout' with you. Isn't that nice?"

"But—"

Actually, the sucker wasn't too bad, extremely bony but rather tasteless, which sometimes is the best you can ask for.

As so often happens, catching that one fish turned Vile into a fisherman for life. Once a goony and irritating kid, he eventually matured into, well, yes, a goony and irritating adult, as often proves to be the case. For thirty years and more, Vile would still visit Idaho every summer and expect me to take him fishing. Hey, that was okay by me. What are cousins for, anyway?

"Don't you dare pull any of your mean little tricks on Vile again this year," Mom would say, tapping her thimble menacingly on the handle of her walker. Odd how a mother will form an impression of her son and never let go of it.

Real Work

First Job

Sometime early in the summer of 1949, when I was six-teen, I casually suggested to my mother that she might advance me a dollar against some future chore. She always feigned hilarity at this bit of audacity from her son, this display of futile hope. Leaning against the kitchen wall, she wiped away tears of mirth with her apron, and then replied, sympathetically but firmly, "Not a chance."

This came as no great shock to me. I had made the request mostly as a lark, figuring what the heck, it's worth a shot. A youth of today might think my mother extraordinarily tight-fisted in refusing me such a paltry sum, but back in those days a family of four could live for a week on a dollar, and often did. That same youth might also think I am writing of a time and place of grinding poverty, but I'm not. In many ways, it was a boom economy, at least for a kid.

It seems to me as if almost everything back then cost fifteen cents: a loaf of bread, a dozen eggs, a pound of bacon, a quart of milk, a bag of dried beans, a gallon of gas, a movie, etc. I don't know why fifteen was the magic number, but it was. If you wanted to splurge in a restaurant, as my family did once every other leap year, you could order yourself a T-bone steak dinner with all the fixings for thirty-five cents, but fifteen cents was the rule for most things. A kid could prosper in that economy. Ages ten through fifteen, I delivered about fifty newspapers a day six days a week on my paper route. The newspaper publisher had indicated that a paper route, "your own little business," as he referred to it, would bring me sizable profits, teach me all about business management, keep me healthy and physically fit, and improve my character to boot. In the five years I delivered papers, my mother said she was pleased with the money I earned from running "my own little business," but that she hadn't detected even a slight improvement in my character. In that regard, she felt the publisher shouldn't make promises he couldn't deliver on.

My newspaper profit worked out to a penny a day per subscriber, or about eight dollars a month, after subtracting the money my customers beat me out of with a variety of scams, the favorite being simply to move away in the dark of night, leaving my bill unpaid. A sophisticated alarm system must have alerted all the members of the Secret Society to Defraud Newspaper Delivery Boys of my imminent attempt to collect from them, because the timing of their departure was often perfect. They waited just long enough to snatch up one last paper from me and then made for the hills. These miscreants assumed that the giant newspaper corporation could afford the loss, but, because of some oversight by the publisher, the loss stopped with the paperboy. No doubt the publisher would have corrected this oversight, if only I could have found some way to bring it to his attention, but it's possible, also, that this was one of the lessons I was supposed to learn from running "my own little business."

I supplemented my paper-route profits by picking up "empties," beer bottles tossed into the ditches by motorists, and returning them for the deposit. Local taverns and stores paid me a half cent for "stubbies" and a full cent for "long-necks" and pop bottles. When the snow finally melted out of the ditches after a long winter, I'd hit the mother lode of emp-ties. For a couple of weeks, I lived high on the hog from the largess heaped upon me by my kindly motorized benefactors, people who drank and drove. Another source of income briefly arose when local farmers offered to pay a penny for each Canadian thistle pulled on their property and brought in as evidence in order to collect the bounty. I liked to think of myself as a bounty hunter arriving at the sheriff's office with the bad guys slung over a horse, except in my case it happened to be with thistles slung over a little red wagon. Bounty hunting for thistles provided a nice means of putting together some quick emergency funds. If you wanted to go to a movie, you could race around a neighboring farm and in no more than an hour seek out and pull at least fifteen thistles. For years the Saturday matinee at the Pandora cost the equivalent of nine thistles for anyone under age twelve. (The theater wouldn't accept the actual thistles, however.) Then Leo Butts got caught hauling in the same thistles multiple times to multiple farmers. Leo The Grifter brought the same batch around so many times, one farmer said he had started to become familiar with individual thistles, had begun to rec-ognize distinctive characteristics and personalities among them, and he said that if Leo had brought the thistles around even one more time, he feared he might develop an affection for them and thus be prevented from throwing them on the fire. Because of Butts's criminal activity, all of us bounty hunters became suspect, and the bottom instantly fell out of the thistle market.

As can be seen from the above numbers, even a kid of eight in those years could scrape together a fairly decent income. Perhaps that is why the concept of allowances remained virtually unknown among my friends and associates, except possibly from the movies, where such a ridiculous notion as parents' giving weekly allowances to their offspring seemed almost commonplace. These absurdities were always good for a laugh at our local theater, particularly among the parents. It's possible that even in our less-than-thriving county there may have been kids from wealthy families lolling about on the parental dole, but none dumb enough to mention it to me or my friends. Had a boy done so he would instantly have become the target of scorn and ridicule and mockery, and of an envy so intense as to eat holes in a person's psyche.

The above introduction to childhood economics of northern Idaho in the summer of 1949 is presented here for the purpose of putting into perspective the great wealth soon to befall me as I stumbled blindly into a new form of economic existence—Real Work.

"Not a chance," my mother repeated that day in the kitchen, still wiping her eyes. "But you know what? I heard that Mr. Gutman is looking for some hired help on his farm. You might see if he has something for you."

"Mr. Gutman? Wonder what he wants done."

"Knowing Mr. Gutman as I do, I think you can be assured it will be real work."

Real Work. The words had a nice ring to them. Real Work might mean Real Money. Within seconds I was on my bike, pedaling the three miles to the Gutman farm. I found Mr. Gutman in his workshop sharpening an ax on a grindstone. He was a huge man, dressed in faded but immaculate bib overalls and shaped vaguely like a turnip with extremities. I was pleased to see I had beaten the crowd that surely must be rushing to land a job with Mr. Gutman. He didn't seem happy to see me.

"Vaht you vant?" he growled, now using a hand file to put razor-sharp edges on the double-bitted ax. To judge from the treatment given his ax, Mr. Gutman took excellent, even excessive, care of his tools. The smooth hickory handle, obviously having received regular rubdowns with linseed oil, glowed softly in the morning light, as might a piece of prized hardwood furniture.

"I'm here about the job."

"Bah! You too young, too puny. I vant real man, do real vork. I fire last two und dey men twice your size, tree times your age. Two big lazy vimps, dey vas. You go home now to your mommer und don't bodder me no more."

"I can do real work," I said. I'd heard of real work, but had never actually done any. Still, how hard could it be? Gutman lifted the file from his ax and squinted at me.

"So you tink you can do real vork, do you? Maybe I give you little test. Grab dat shovel und come mit me." He leaned the ax against the grindstone and strode out the door. As I followed behind, I glanced around, looking for signs of my competitors streaming in to beat me out of the Gutman job. Odd, I thought. I must be the only person who knows about it. What a stroke of luck!

We presently arrived at a shed approximately twenty feet square. It had two windows and a door on the front. A large door at the rear opened on the barnyard and apparently was intended for the removal of animal waste product. Gutman pointed down at a mysterious but obviously crude substance covering the floor. This was not something you would expect on the Gutman farm, which otherwise was tidy in all respects. He would never have allowed such a disgusting accumulation ever to occur on one of his floors. The substance, covering the floor to a depth of about one foot, defied identification. My guess is that the previous owner had used the shed to house young pigs for a month or two each year. The farmer first deposited a layer of straw, and then the pigs deposited what they could, and then came another layer of straw, and so on. He repeated this process year after year without ever bothering to clean out the straw and residue of pig. Time, heat, and the pressure of hundreds of little hooves produced an almost geological process that fused multiple layers of straw and pig manure into a mystery material that appeared to me, and I think also to Gutman, to be virtually indestructible.

"Ha! Now ve see if you man enough to do real vork," Gutman said, a chuckle rippling through his turnip body. "I go to town soon. Ven I get back, I see vaht kind job you do on shed floor." His eyes twinkled with evil merriment. "You got shed cleaned up, you got job. Man's wages. One dollar an hour. Understand?"

"Yes, sir."

I watched Gutman's pickup truck disappear down the highway toward town. Then I turned back to the shed and studied the mystery substance. It appeared to be a single, great, irreducible slab. Picking up the shovel, I gave the slab a few tentative jabs. Not only didn't the shovel make a dent, it bounced off. I sat down on the step to think. Was Gutman serious? Was this a joke? Or was this what was meant by "real work."

When Gutman returned late that afternoon, I was still sitting on the shed step.

"Vaht!" he exclaimed. "You still here? I told you I don't vant you hangin' around boddering me no more. Go home to your mommer!" He walked over and looked in the shed.

It had been cleaned right down to the concrete floor.

Gutman obviously couldn't believe what he saw, and in particular he couldn't believe that I had done it. "Show me hands."

I held up my hands. They were a mass of broken blisters, although they didn't hurt all that much, unless I looked at them. One of the two lessons I learned that day was that whenever you go after a job of real work, take gloves. You never know, you might get it.

Gutman took hold of the tips of my fingers with his own thick, hard hands. He nodded approvingly. "Goot," he said.

"Don't vorry, dey not ruined forever. Vill harden up in a day or two."

Again he looked around the shed, perhaps wondering about the marks of a grid in the concrete floor. "It could be better in corners," he said, frowning critically. Then he said, "You start tomorrow at eight sharp. Don't be late. Or I fire you."

I took the warning as a compliment. My status had improved from that of being sent home to my mommer to being fired.

After remembering to bring gloves, the second great lesson I learned that day about real work is that there's a lot to be said for just getting the job done, no matter how you manage to do it. It has been my experience in later years that there are so many people who can't seem to get the job done that those who can become prized employees on that count alone, no matter their other shortcomings: "Sure, old Fred turned out to be a serial killer, an arsonist, a thief, and a pornographer, but I'll say this for him, he knew how to get the job done."

Gutman was a hard man to work for. Scarcely a day went by that he didn't scream at me for something, usually for failing to measure up to the high level of excellence he demanded. Over the summer he fired me at least three times but then showed up at my house the next morning to hire me back.

One of the things Gutman fired me for was a lapse in counting. One day we were out dynamiting stumps, which is not only real work but a lot of fun. Gutman enjoyed it as much as I did. He and I placed dynamite under a row of ten stumps, after which I walked off to a safe distance while Gutman ran along the row and lit the fuses. Then he retreated over to me, panting heavily, and gasped out, "You count blasts." The reason for counting blasts, of course, was to make sure that all the stumps had exploded before you walked over and started to examine them. I felt both pleased and uneasy that Gutman would entrust me with such a serious responsibility. My task was simple enough, a first grader could do it, as Gutman later commented, but because an explosion can be a terrible distraction, I repeated to myself, "Got to remember to count the blasts, got to remember to count the blasts, got to remember . . ." And then the first stump went up with a brain-rattling explosion. I immediately forgot to count the blasts. I never even got to "one."

Suddenly the series of blasts ended. "Dat ten?" Gutman asked.

"Uh, ten?"

"Ten. Goot. I go check—"

KABLAAAMMMM!

"Gott in himmel!"

"No, see, as I was saying, Mr. Gutman, that other one was nine. This here one was ten!"

"You fired!"

Gutman loved dynamite. One day he and I were standing on a hill looking down at a picturesque little creek that meandered through his meadow. The longer Gutman looked at it, the more the little creek irritated him. It was, in his view, fooling around, a crime he often accused me of and sometimes fired me for. He went into town and came back with a box of ditching dynamite. By this time I had used a steel rod to punch a row of holes in the soft ground between the meanders. Gutman placed a stick of dynamite in each hole. The nice thing about ditching dynamite is that the concussion from one detonation sets off the next stick in the row and so on. In one explosive roar, the dynamite ripped open the ground as if by a gigantic zipper. Instantly, Gutman's creek cleaned up its act and ran in a straight line. He seemed pleased. Personally, I preferred the creek when it meandered, but I kept my opinion to myself. Gutman was not a person with whom I wanted to get into a discussion of aesthetics.

I spent far more time that summer in the company of Gutman than I did with my family and friends, and I learned an important lesson about real work. It's basically pretty unpleasant, even though you're paid real money for it. Still, there is a satisfaction to it that goes beyond mere money earned, and it comes from the knowledge that you can do real work. Without the money, of course, forget it. Nobody does real work for the satisfaction.

My main job for Gutman was to build fences, and by the end of the summer I had built new barbed-wire fences around almost all his property. Every time I thought I was almost done with fencing, he would buy the farm next to him or another piece of property, and I would be off again building fence. By the end of the summer, I had become an efficient and skilled builder of fences, even if I did say so myself. I would have had to say so myself, because Gutman never would. In all the time I worked for him, not once did I get a compliment. On the other hand, simply not getting permanently fired by Gutman was a major compliment in itself. Anyone who had ever worked for him would have said so, and I eventually came to recognize this and took a measure of pride in it. I was forty-five years old by then, but it was still something worth recognizing.

There was an occasional sign, though, that Gutman actually liked me. One day he thought he had killed me, and flew into a great panic. I was tearing out an old barbed-wire fence, while Gutman worked a hundred yards or so away from me with his bulldozer. It was terribly hot, and I was tired and thirsty, so I walked over to a little tree, flopped down in its shade, and took a drink from my jug of water. At that moment, Gutman accidentally backed the bulldozer into the fence. Three strands of barbed wire and a dozen posts were snapped forward and fifty feet into the air for practically a quarter of a mile. Anyone standing next to it might have been sawed into four neat sections by the barbs. Seconds later Gutman came tearing out of the woods, looking for my remains, which happened to be sitting under a tree sipping water and thinking, Hey, maybe he actually cares. Relieved to see me in one piece instead of four, Gutman still wasn't pleased to see me relaxing in the shade of the little tree, even though this supported his conviction that it was my standard practice every time I was out of his sight. "You scare me to death for notting! It lucky ting you loafing under tree instead of vorking! Whew! What a relief! You fired!"

Whatever my complaints about Gutman as my very first employer, he did something for me that not my parents, not my grandparents, not my aunts and uncles, not my teachers, not the nuns or priests, not anyone else had ever done for me. He made me rich. I now made more money in a single day than I profited from in a whole month of delivering newspapers. I made as much money as my stepfather, who besides laboring on our small farm also worked for a hardware store in town to support the family. I, on the other hand, had no overhead, no wife, no kids, no car, no house, no insurance, no taxes, no doctors, no lawyers. All I had was pure money, paid to me promptly, if somewhat begrudgingly, by Gutman every Saturday at five o'clock in the afternoon, all in crisp bills. By rich I mean I could take a girl out for Cokes, hamburgers, fries, and a movie with popcorn and candy, and still have change left over from a dollar. I even saved most of that dollar, because I didn't have a girl to take out anyhow. (I was still so young and innocent I didn't realize that being rich could easily solve that problem.) Absurd though it is even to think about, I could have taken one of my dollars and bought for the family a loaf of bread, a dozen eggs, a pound of bacon, a quart of milk, a bag of dried beans, a gallon of gas, and still had change. Such a ridiculous notion never occurred to me, of course, as I greedily amassed more wealth than I had ever seen and quite possibly even more than my mother and stepfather had ever seen. In some ways, I think I never saw that kind of wealth again. For that one brief moment in time, I felt rich. I have never felt rich since. There were other satisfactions, too, of course, such as when my mother occasionally asked to borrow a dollar. I never mastered the feigned hilarity with which she had once greeted my own such requests, but I could make a reasonable show of it. Mom said so herself, even as her fingers nimbly extracted the dollar from my stash.

Although I could never bring myself to like Gutman, and he never gave any sign that was one of his ultimate concerns, there was one little topic that I expected him to bring up sometime, probably during one of the rages I inspired in him, but he never did. I had to like him for that, for never once mentioning his ax, the well-honed ax, his favorite ax, the ax I had used to chop the mystery substance of the pig shed into neat little one-foot cubes, which could then be easily pried up with the shovel and flung out the back door of the shed. I doubt he ever again cut wood with that ax, nor perhaps could have, but maybe he hung it up someplace, gave it some kind of honorable retirement. It could certainly still have served as a wall ornament, a conversation piece, maybe even as some kind of weird trophy for his good judgment in hiring persons to do real work: "You see dat ax? Vell, vun time dis schrimpy kid showed up hier und . . ."

About the Author

Patrick F. McManus has written eleven collections of essays, four other books, and two plays. There are nearly two million copies of his books in print, including the bestselling *They Shoot Canoes, Don't They?*, *The Night the Bear Ate Goombaw*, and *A Fine and Pleasant Misery*. He divides his time between Spokane, Washington, and Idaho.